Borderline Personality Disorder

Improve Your Social Skills With Overcoming Depression

(A Comprehensive Guide to Learn About the Borderline Personality Disorder)

Michael Larsen

Published By **Oliver Leish**

Michael Larsen

All Rights Reserved

*Borderline Personality Disorder: Improve Your
Social Skills With Overcoming Depression (A
Comprehensive Guide to Learn About the
Borderline Personality Disorder)*

ISBN   978-0-9938301-4-3

No part of this guidebook shall be reproduced in any form without permission in writing from the publisher except in the case of brief quotations embodied in critical articles or reviews.

Legal & Disclaimer

Table Of Contents

Chapter 1: What Is Borderline Personality Disorder (Bpd)?

Symptoms of Borderline Personality Disorder

People with BPD revel in huge mood swings and may enjoy instability and lack of self assurance. Borderline Personality Disorder influences the way you enjoy about your self, the way you relate to others, and the way you're treated. Not everybody evaluations borderline individual disease.

Borderline Personality Disorder (BPD) patients can revel in mood swings and feature uncertainty about how they view themselves and their function inside the worldwide.

Borderline persona disease patients additionally need to look matters again and again, like numerous correct or lousy. Other human beings's critiques approximately them can trade all of sudden. An character who's regarded as a chum in the end can be taken into consideration an enemy the other day or a traitor.

These changing feelings can bring about excessive and unstable relationships. Some human beings revel in only a few signs and symptoms and signs and symptoms, at the same time as others have many symptoms and signs. Symptoms can be introduced about with the aid of the use of reputedly not unusual occurrences. For example, sufferers of borderline personality contamination may be irritated and disillusioned at the slightest separation from human beings they experience close to, along with journeying on business enterprise trips.

Depending on the severity and frequency of signs and their age and their infection, how lengthy they remaining. According to the Diagnostic and Statistical Manual Diagnostic Framework, a number of the most signs and symptoms and symptoms may additionally moreover encompass:

Great efforts through way of friends and circle of relatives to avoid giving up real or imaginary.

Unstable private relationships that change among ideologies such as;

"I'm in love!"

"I hate it"

This is now and again referred to as "division".

Great practices that might have risky results, which incorporates excessive spending, volatile intercourse, substance abuse or reckless the use of.

Severe despair, irritability or tension can also closing for a few hours to a few days.

Chronic feelings of anger or vacancy.

Inappropriate, severe or uncontrollable anger .This - often observed thru shame and guilt.

Irrational Feelings your Disconnected out of your very own mind or feelings of identity, or "out of body" feelings of tension and pressure related to strain. Severe episodes of stress can also bring about quick intellectual episodes.

Taking excessive steps to avoid severe fear of departure, even actual or imagined separation or rejection.

Rapid adjustments in self-identity and self-picture that contain converting dreams and values, and making your self experience horrible or as in case you not exist.

Stress-associated paranoia and intervals of touch with truth, from a few minutes to a few hours

Safeguarding fulfillment thru influencing and treating volatile behaviors, along with gambling, reckless using, risky intercourse, spousal, binge eating or drug use, or leaving a outstanding task or finishing a terrific relationship.

In reaction to the dangers of suicide or the priority of being treated or harm, often separated or rejected.

Extensive mode lasts from some hours to three days, that could embody excessive pride, irritability, embarrassment or tension.

The ongoing emotions of emptiness

Inappropriate, intense anger, which encompass repeated lack of temper, sarcasm or bitterness, or physical battle of words.

Attempts to avoid giving up real or imagined, including starting an intimate (physical or emotional) relationship or hoping to interrupt off contact with someone

Impressive and often dangerous behaviors, along with spending problems, having unprotected intercourse, substance abuse, reckless the use of, and ingesting ingredients. If this conduct takes location in most instances during a excessive temper or electricity length, this mode may be a symptom of a contamination - no longer a disturbance of the reputation quo.

Frequent mind of suicidal behavior or threats

Severe and noticeably variable mode with each event lasting from a few hours to three days

Chronic emotions of vacancy

Inappropriate, severe anger or hassle controlling anger

Hard to believe, this is every so often with irrational fear of different human beings's intentions

Feelings of customization, which include the sensation of being reduce off from your self, seeing your self from out of doors one's body, or the feeling of being unrealistic

Explained Symptoms

Because of the priority that one-of-a-kind humans will abandon them. Because of this, they are able to leave those who cannot depart other humans - in conditions while distinct people will now not feel it or take it in my view.

The Borderline Personality Disorder is characterised through emotional disorder, which means that a proper away, repetitive, and demanding mood this is beyond the manage of the sufferer. This trouble makes it difficult for people with a hassle to form and hold relationships. They furthermore face difficulties in controlling their very personal disorderly and careless conduct and often provide you with thoughts approximately who they will be.

The everyday subject matter of this illness is rapid and sudden adjustments in someone's mind, moods, behaviors, relationships and ideals. Often, those fast changes are due to repeated fears of being criticized or irritated with the useful useful resource of numerous humans, or they'll be created with the aid of using one of a kind human beings's actions that experience like grievance, including small versions or Changes in plans.

In reaction to those forms of situations, someone suffering from borderline personality ailment may additionally abruptly turn out to be very unhappy, nervous, irritated, or in a moody temper. The character can also workout self-harming behaviors, including decreasing yourself off, or sporting out suicide. Unfortunately, these character patterns frequently reason distress in a single's relationships, art work, and wonderful social situations, that is why they may take delivery of a personality sickness.

People who be afflicted by means of borderline persona ailment often have a records of severe relationships that begin and save you very all of sudden. Often, this is because of matters:

Their fear of being abandoned

Their tendency to scold short after which to criticize extraordinary human beings

For example, a pupil who became laid low with borderline persona ailment brief formed a deep bond with each other student whom she met in magnificence. Immediately, the more youthful lady desired to spend all her loose time with a few other pupil and communicate masses approximately her new "notable pal."

However, for the primary time even as some other scholar refused to offer to be social, the younger lady changed into terrified and harm. He suspected that his new buddy became leaving him and beat up some other student, beat him and accused his buddy of leaving him. Understandably, the opportunity scholar ended the relationship.

For the ones suffering with borderline character disorder, such episodes rise up regularly and can be overwhelming. Severe emotions which consist of fear, misery, tension, anger, sadness and embarrassment can persist for some hours as long as they'll remaining for a few days.

In reaction to leaving or feeling damage, the offending person makes some thing instead (or as a substitute threatening to do) in an try and save you the opportunity individual from leaving. Using the preceding example, a borderline personality scholar starts offevolved over and over calling her friend in an try to convince her to keep the relationship.

However, at the identical time as human beings are irritated and overwhelmed, sufferers of borderline person infection additionally hesitate. Some human beings engage in obligations which include decreasing their legs and arms and one-of-a-type types of suicide. People may moreover have interaction in the following:

Drugs & Alcohol excessively

Engage in unstable sexual encounters

Shopping they cannot discover the cash for

Gamble excessively

Having unstable ingesting conduct

Benching & Cleaning

In more irritating situations, the character may additionally additionally try to dedicate suicide or reflect onconsideration on suicide in element. Most human beings concerned on this trouble are continuously attempting out their very personal relationships for problems and assume to be deserted by means of way of manner of different human beings. They want to categorize themselves, others, and topics into any "all right" or "all terrible" instructions and not the use of a center ground.

This is why small problems can often bring about the prevent of a courting. Yet, in spite of ways fast their relationship ends, many humans laid low with borderline person disease are honestly afraid of being lonely because of the reality they assume they're unable to address the issues themselves. Borderline character illness in fight may be very tiring and disturbing.

People with this hassle suffer from extreme bodily, emotional and intellectual ache at all times. They aren't even sure who they'll be. In one minute the man or woman can don't forget himself as a high-quality person, and in the next minute he is going to recollect himself as terrible and bad. Thoughts about different human beings additionally vary unexpectedly. That man or woman wants to accept as true with others, however at the equal time, he does no longer anticipate extremely good humans are sincere. All this confusion can without hassle make someone feels:

Empty

Sad

Hollow

With the aggravation of disturbances, human beings suffering with borderline character infection every so often experience like they depart their our our bodies in times of pressure and can't hold in mind what came about. These immoderate intervals of loneliness first-class growth the unstable feeling in their self. Likewise, and further traumatic, there may be a duration of deception that could arise for the duration of times of strain or despair.

Having relationships which might be strangely immoderate and risky (which encompass being someone else's ideal, then disliking them significantly). Being very uncertain about your self - no longer virtually expertise who they're or what to consider yourself. May be dangerous (e.G. Cash earlier than spending money, volatile sexual conduct, use of risky pills or alcohol, reckless using or consuming bananas) or appearing indecently.

Repeated self-harm, suicide, or talking and considering suicide. Experiencing times of brief lived but severe emotional 'low' or irritability or tension. This is generally best for some hours at a time, however from time to time it is able to very last longer. To experience the steady feeling of being 'empty' from internal.

Experiencing anger this is fairly immoderate, and in percent to what triggers anger, and being no longer able to triumph over it (which consist of getting a temper or preventing a combat). When under pressure, others may moreover revel in excessive doubts or unusual feelings of being separated from their emotions, body or surroundings. There are a few described signs of Borderline Personality Disorder that are given below:

Fear of giving up

Unstable Relationships

Blurring or changing your photo

Poor Self-treating

Self-Harming

Highly Emotional Swings

Chronic emotions of emptiness

Explosive Temper

Suspicious or out of contact with reality

a. Fear of giving up

People with BPD often sense abandoned or lonely. Even a few thing unpleasant, collectively with a cherished one arriving home overdue or happening a weekend, is in dire worry. This can be a drastic try and keep the opposite person near.

You can beg, kiss, start preventing with each distinct, song your lady friend's movements, or bodily stop this person from leaving. Unfortunately, this behavior has the opposite have an impact on others sending others away.

b. Unstable relationship

People with BPD have relationships which can be excessive and brief-lived. You may moreover quick be in love, believing that each new man or woman is a few element an top notch manner to make you feel wholesome, truely to be disappointed.

Your relationships appearance ideal or excellent, without any center ground. Your cherished ones, friends, or circle of relatives individuals can also moreover moreover experience that they have end up emotional because of your swinging from best to lack of appreciation, anger and hatred.

c. Blurring or changing your picture

When you have got got BPD, your feeling is commonly unstable. Sometimes you may sense appropriate about your self, but particular times you hate yourself, or perhaps suppose your self evil.

You have no clean idea of who you're or what you need in life. As a surrender result, you could often change jobs, pals, lovers, religion, values, desires, or even sexual identity.

d. Poor Self-treating

Turn around, deal with your self destructively. If you have got were given BPD, you may have interaction in unstable, sensation-on the lookout for behaviors, specifically at the same time as you are disillusioned.

You can spend cash you cannot locate the money for, devour, pressure carelessly, boom a store and interact in volatile intercourse, or abuse capsules or alcohol. These unstable behaviors assist you to experience higher inside the second, but it could hurt you and people spherical you.

e. Self-Harming

Self-harming conduct that also entails suicide threats or attempts. It is common for people with BPD to devote suicidal and planned self-harm. Suicidal behavior includes considering suicide, making pointers or threats of suicide, or simply attempting suicide.

Self-harm consists of all certainly one of a type tries to damage yourself with out the motive of suicide. Common kinds of self-damage embody biting and burning.

f. Highly Emotional Swings

Unstable emotions and moods are not unusual with BPD. For a second, you can revel in the satisfaction, and the following, the frustration. The little matters that distinctive people brush can deliver you into an emotional tail spin.

These temper swings are excessive, but they depart rapid (no longer like the emotional swings of depression or bipolar ailment), commonly lasting only a few mins or hours.

g. Chronic emotions of vacancy

People with BPD often speak about being empty, as if there has been a hole or a vacuum inner them. This feeling is burdened, so you can try to fill the void with pills, food, or sex. But now not something is certainly pleasing.

h. Explosive Temper

If you have got were given BPD, you could warfare with intense anger and a quick mood. You may also have hassle controlling your self as soon as the fuse is lit. It is crucial to be aware that this anger does now not continuously exit. You can spend a whole lot of time feeling angry approximately yourself.

i. Suspicious or out of contact with truth

People with BPD often struggle with skeptics or doubtful mind approximately the motive of others. When under stress, you may even lose contact with reality. You may additionally moreover sense foggy, faraway, or revel in like you are from your body.

Causes of Borderline Personality Disorder

The reason for the borderline individual illness is not but clean, however studies indicates that genetics, intellectual shape and characteristic, and environmental, cultural and social elements play a characteristic, or that character troubles are at stake.

The actual motives of borderline character disease are not acknowledged, however maximum possibly it is the end result of organic, highbrow and social risk elements. In modern-day-day, such individual problems are more likely to be inherited because of influential genetic elements affecting families.

Some individual tendencies, which incorporates emotional instability, also are inherited. Using thoughts imaging era, researchers have determined that effective behaviors related to seizure-related persona sickness, together with impulsivity, are related to lower tiers of thoughts chemical serotonin.

Using comparable techniques, researchers also placed that patients of Borderline Personality Disorder have a greater impact on deciphering human beings's faces on the same time as in comparison to people with out distraction. This makes it tough for some people to interpret impartial facial expressions, and once in a while it causes them to misinterpret independent faces, which includes threatening ones. In addition, a few mind imaging studies have located that folks that diagnose individual problems to some extent display off small period in positive areas of the brain worried in emotional functioning.

The most alarming studies findings have related borderline individual sickness to abuse history, specially sexual, physical, emotional, and verbal abuse. In one observe, ninety one percent of the patients had been abused and ninety two percent had been critically unnoticed in early life. In each distinctive have a take a look at, 40% were sexually assaulted, affecting both ladies and men. In many times, the patients noted sexual and bodily abuse as youngsters with the aid of more than one character.

In some other file, 50% of people stated having a Borderline Personality Disorder (BPD) that sexually assaulted kids on a weekly foundation for at least three hundred and sixty five days through a determine or family buddy. In this equal check, it changed into observed that the severity of sexual abuse and regular forget is associated with the severity of this sickness.

One precept suggests that people who develop troubles are glaringly evidence towards emotional reactions and cannot reply in a wholesome and supportive manner to emotional opinions.

Then the hazard is further exacerbated even as this man or woman is located in a state of abuse, as has just been described. Similarly, as kids broaden up with abusive dad and mom who constantly criticize them and reject their emotions, it is not tough to assume why they will be so stressed approximately their emotional reactions. There can be doubts.

May boom the risk of being born. Although those elements may additionally additionally growth a person's hazard, this does not suggest that the individual might be much more likely to disrupt individual. Likewise, there can be human beings without risk elements who will boom a borderline individual illness of their lives.

The reasons for BPD are uncertain. But as with maximum situations, BPD is characterized with the resource of a mixture of genetic and environmental factors.

Traumatic events that occur in younger humans are associated with growing BPD. Many human beings with BPD will revel in parental forget about about or physical, sexual or emotional abuse in their childhood. The reasons of BPD have not been honestly understood, but scientists agree that this is the give up result of a mixture of things, which incorporates:

Genetics

Environmental Factors

Brain Function or Abnormalities

(a) Genetics

Although no unique gene or gene profile has been proven to right away purpose BPD, research indicates that near family contributors with BPD can be at higher hazard for growing problems.

People with near family human beings, collectively with dad and mom or siblings, can be at greater danger of growing character problems.

(b)   Environmental Factors

Many humans with borderline personality illness report worrying life sports, which includes adolescence abuse, abandonment, or tension. Others can also have had volatile, illicit members of the family and mutual conflicts.

(c) Brain Function or Abnormalities

Emotional law may be special in humans with BPD, suggesting that a few signs and symptoms and signs and symptoms have a neurological basis. In particular, the additives of the thoughts that manipulate emotions and choice-making or choice-making can not speak properly with each different.

Some studies has confirmed adjustments in effective regions of the mind, which incorporates emotion law, aggression and aggression. In addition, a few mind chemical substances that assist alter temper, which include serotonin, won't feature nicely. Studies show that people with borderline individual disorder may also want to make structural and practical modifications in the thoughts, specifically in areas that manage impulse and emotional regulation.

But is it now not clean whether or not or now not the ones changes are a purpose of the sickness, or a reason of the contamination. There are numerous complex subjects taking place inside the BPD brain, and researchers are however decided to be powerful. Things make you revel in greater scary and worrying than wonderful humans.

Your Fight or Flight transfer journeys effects, and after it runs, it hijacks your rational mind, giving transport to survivors that are not constantly worthwhile. It ought to make it sound like you have got nothing. After all, what are you able to do if you have a one-of-a-type mind? But the truth is, you may alternate your thoughts.

Every time you have a look at a ultra-modern competing reaction or a chilled approach you're growing new nerve pathways. Some treatments, together with mindfulness meditation, also can beautify your intellectual health. And as you exercise, the ones paths becomes more potent and greater computerized. So do no longer surrender! With time and energy of will, you could trade your way of thinking, feeling and walking.

Treatment & Diagnose of Borderline Personality Disorder

There is not any unique examination or treatment for BPD. Speaking and expertise approximately a person can most effective be identified via a highbrow health expert. BPD may be identified if someone has a couple of signs and symptoms and signs and symptoms or signs and symptoms and signs. There are many combos of those abilities, so human beings diagnosed with BPD may additionally understand some component very unique.

If someone has a BPD symptom, their medical clinical medical doctor or psychologist will cautiously ask questions about their life, studies and symptoms in advance than developing a analysis. It also can moreover take more than one consultation to just accept as proper with this diagnosis, as some signs of BPD are just like signs of numerous intellectual fitness situations.

As we understand, there is no definitive clinical take a look at for the prognosis of BPD, and the prognosis isn't always primarily based on a particular symptom or symptom. After a comprehensive scientific interview, highbrow fitness experts have the excellent prognosis of BPD, which incorporates talking to previous therapists, reviewing preceding scientific studies and on the same time as appropriate, interviews with buddies and circle of relatives.

Borderline individual illness has historically been considered difficult to cope with. But, with new, proof-based totally remedies, many humans with troubles revel in greater or less intense signs and signs, and a better high-quality of existence. It is important that victims of Borderline Personality Disorder are looking for proof-based totally, specialised remedy from a properly expert organisation.

Other forms of treatment, or remedies furnished via manner of the usage of a scientific doctor or therapist that aren't well professional, may not gain this individual. Many factors take a long term to beautify signs and symptoms and signs after remedy begins offevolved, so it's far essential that patients and their cherished ones be afflicted by borderline person disorder and gather appropriate resource within the route of treatment.

Borderline man or woman illness regularly accompanies specific intellectual ailments. It may be tough to diagnose the ailment and cope with pretty various person problems, particularly if the symptoms of other illnesses exceed the signs and symptoms and signs of personality disease.

For instance, a person affected by borderline personality illness may also be more likely to experience despair, bipolar disorder, tension problems, substance use problems, or eating problems.

Some Treatments

With remedy, most humans with BPD get over their signs and signs and symptoms inside the shortest feasible time. If there is a notable risk of recuperation, they may now not purpose the signs and symptoms and signs another time.

Most human beings locate that their signs and symptoms beautify internal a few years after analysis. Many human beings have a superb social lifestyles and paintings lifestyles. Some people nevertheless face a few troubles at artwork and in social life, despite the fact that their signs and symptoms have advanced. An effective remedy plan have to encompass your priorities, in addition to any other facilities you can have.

Examples of treatment remedy embody psychotherapy. Medicines, groups, peer and circle of relatives assist. The important motive of the remedy is to instruct a person with BPD on their very very own treatment as speedy as they examine what works and what should now not.

Psychotherapy

Meditations

(a) Psychotherapy

Psychotherapy which is also known as talk therapy is the notable manner to cope with BPD. These remedies normally embody talking to as a minimum one-on-one health experts, or now and again turning into a member of special organizations.

BPD is the number one line of desire for psychiatric behavioral remedy (DBT), Cognitive Behavioral Therapy (CBT) and

Psychodynamic Psychotherapy (PP). Learning methods to treatment emotional dysregulation in treatment is frequently the crucial thing to extended-time period development for those with BPD.

Pseudo treatment is a primary line treatment for people with borderline character disorder. A clinical health practitioner can provide one-to-one remedy among a clinical health practitioner and a affected person, or deal with in a fixed placing. P

Hysician-led institution training can assist human beings with borderline personality ailment learn how to engage with others and efficiently specific themselves. It is essential that remedy people live with you, and accept as true with your therapist.

The nature of borderline personality disorder could make it difficult for humans with an infection to keep a comfortable and trusting dating with their health practitioner. Borderline is used to deal with personality infection in two examples of psychotherapy.

Diabetic Behavior Therapy (DBT)

Cognitive Behavioral Therapy (CBT)

i. Diabetic Behavior Therapy (DBT)

This shape of treatment changed into evolved for those who be troubled by borderline personality disorder. The DBT makes use of principles of mindfulness and reputation or is conscious and privy to the contemporary state of affairs and emotional nation. DBT offers us a few suitable skills that could help us hundreds as a way to:

Overcome immoderate feelings

Reduce self-poor behaviors and beautify relationships

ii. Cognitive Behavioral Therapy (CBT)

This kind of remedy lets in humans to end up aware of and trade underlying beliefs and behaviors that find out misconceptions about themselves and others, and the difficulty in communicating with others. CBT can help alleviate a number of mood and tension symptoms and signs and symptoms and symptoms and decrease the great form of suicidal or self-harming behaviors.

(b)   Meditations

Med drugs can be beneficial for healing plans, however there can be no unique drug for treating the underlying symptoms and symptoms of BPD. In addition, many drug remedies can be used with labels of labels to treat numerous signs and signs and symptoms. And for some people, low-dose antipsychotic pills can help manipulate signs and symptoms and signs, which include atypical thinking.

Treatment with tablets may additionally require the care of more than one clinical expert. Some drug remedies can purpose precise facet outcomes in different people. Talk to your medical health practitioner approximately what to anticipate with a selected remedy.

Because the benefits are uncertain, capsules are usually no longer used as a primary treatment for borderline persona sickness. However, in some instances, a psychologist may additionally additionally advise drug treatments for the treatment of unique signs and symptoms and symptoms which consist of:

The temper changes

Mental strain

Other associate highbrow issues

(c) Short-term Hospitaliation

Extreme strain or short-time period hospitalization, can be important to make certain protection. It can help lots to be able to get consolation from Borderline Personality Disorder further to all of the signs and symptoms & consequences take location due to BPD.

Some Self-Helps to overcome Borderline Personality Disorder

When psychologists speak approximately "character," they may be looking for advice from styles of wondering, feeling and behavior that make each mother and father precise. No one is constantly the identical all the time, however we typically generally tend to have interaction and interact with the sector in a very steady manner.

This is why human beings are often described as "embarrassed," "outgoing," "trendy," "fun," and so on. These are elements of character. Since personality is so intrinsically related to identification, the phrase "person sickness" may want to make you experience that there may be a few issue basically incorrect with you.

But personality disorder is not a character choice. In scientific phrases, "character disorder" manner that your method to the world is a terrific deal great than ordinary. (In one in all a type phrases, you do not observe the strategies that most human beings count on).

Of route, they ought to be used to supplement the care of an right therapist and now not on my own. An perfect assignment includes mastering more approximately your very very personal contamination thru self-assist, studying wholesome coping capabilities for BPD, and finding approaches to help you express and manage your feelings.

There are valuable self-help assets available for BPD that can be used on the factor of traditional sorts of remedy. Books and online resources offer statistics about BPD and propose ways to deal with the signs and symptoms.

It motives chronic problems in masses of areas of your life, which include your relationships, career, and your emotions approximately your self and others. There are 3 commonplace guidelines that you could virtually observe to advantage or conquer Borderline Personality Disorder (BPD) & its effects on existence.

Calm the emotional typhoon

Learn to speedy overcome and go through

Improve your mutual or interpersonal abilties

1. Tip # 1: Calm your Emotional Storm

As a person with BPD, you've got possibly spent hundreds of time struggling together together with your thoughts and emotions, so wrap your thoughts spherical it. Acceptance may be a difficult element. But accepting your feelings does no longer mean approving them or resigning your self to ache.

It genuinely method searching for to fight, avoid, suppress or deny what you enjoy. Allowing yourself to have the ones emotions can take away loads in their electricity. Just try to experience your feelings without judgment or complaint. Leave the past and the future and pay precise hobby to the existing moment. Mind-making strategies can be very effective on this regard.

Watch on the move (can also additionally help to recognize them like waves).

Focus at the physical feelings that accompany your emotions.

Remind your self that just due to the truth you feel some thing does not advocate that it's far actual.

(a) Do something that triggers one or more of your senses

Being self-aware is the fastest, easiest way to loosen up yourself. You need to test to discover which sensory stimulus works fantastic for you.

You might also even want unique techniques for awesome modes. What will let you to be angry or angry whilst you grow to be irritated or depressed. Some thoughts, you need to observe in this enjoy:

Touch

Taste

Smell

Sight

Sound

(i)   Touch

If you are not feeling well, attempt on foot bloodless or warm (however now not heat) warm water on your fingers. Grab a chunk of ice; or seize the threshold of an object or piece of furnishings as tightly as you can. If you're feeling overwhelmed, and you need to chill out, attempt a warmth bathtub or shower. Smuggling under the bed cover, or rolling with pets.

(ii)   Taste

If you experience empty and apathetic, attempt sucking on sturdy-flavored mints or candy, or eating a few aspect with a slight taste, which include salt and vinegar chips. If you need to be calm, try some element warmth, which incorporates warm tea or soup.

(iii)   Smells

Brighten the candles, fragrance the vegetation, strive a scent treatment, spritz your favored perfume, or whip up a few thing inside the kitchen that smells. You may locate which you respond outstanding to harsh fragrances, which include citrus, spices, and incense.

(iv)   Sight

Focus on an image that catches your interest. It can be some issue you consider to your at once surroundings (a beautiful view, a lovable floral association, a fave portray or image) or a few issue you could do not forget.

(v)   Sound

Try to pay attention loud noises, sound the alarm, or whistle while you need a shock. To loosen up out, activate the soothing track or concentrate to the soothing sounds of nature, which incorporates the wind, the birds or the ocean. If you cannot listen the actual problem, a legitimate tool works properly.

(b)   Reduce your emotional weakness / vulnerability

When you are below strain and stress, you are much more likely to enjoy bad emotions. This is why it is crucial to attend to your physical and mental fitness. You can resultseasily deal with your self through following those techniques:

Avoid temper changing drug treatments

Eating a balanced, nutritious diet regime

Standard sleep

Exercise regularly

Reduce stress

Following rest strategies

2.   Tip # 2: Learn to fast triumph over and suffer

The calming technique will will let you loosen up at the same time as you start to get off the rails with strain. But what do you do when you have tough emotions?

This is wherein the Borderline Personality Disorder (BPD) is available in. In the midst of this second, you are so decided for treatment that you may do whatever, which embody subjects you understand you want to now not do, reckless intercourse, volatile the usage of, and consuming alcohol.

Being out of manipulate collectively along with your conduct

(a) Being out of manipulate collectively together with your conduct

It is crucial to recognize that this unique .That serves a motive. They are suffering to cope with the problem. They only make you experience higher, in spite of the truth that for just a 2d. But extended-time period charges are immoderate.

Re-controlling your conduct starts offevolved offevolved with studying to deal with the problem. This is the vital component to converting the negative styles of BPD. The capability to cope with anxiety will assist you suppress your pause at the equal time as you want to behave.

Instead of reacting to hard feelings with self-bad behaviors, you may observe to triumph over them on the equal time as being on pinnacle of factors of the enjoy. To triumph over Borderline Personality Disorder similarly to its signs and symptoms and signs and symptoms & consequences, you need to need to:

Stay in contact along facet your emotions

Living emotionally

Manage ugly or intimidating feelings

Be calm and focused even in hard conditions

(b)   In an emergency, engage or distract yourself

If the efforts to calm you aren't jogging and you are starting to feel beaten by means of the use of the usage of the devastating strain, attractive your self can help. All you need to do is reputation your interest sufficient to dispose of the awful impulse.

Anything that catches your interest can art work, however its attention is more powerful whilst the interest is easy. In addition to the senses-primarily based totally techniques cited earlier, there are some subjects you could try:

Watch TV

Throw your self at artwork

Call a Friend

Get Active

Do some aspect that you experience doing

(i)   Watch TV

Choose a few thing you experience is opposite to it: a comedy, a few issue to be cushty if you are feeling sad, or if you are irritated or irritated.

(ii)   Throw your self at paintings

You can also get concerned with the chores and duties of your house: cleansing your house, doing outdoor paintings, grocery buying, getting prepared your puppy or doing laundry.

(iii)   Call a Friend

Talking to someone you accept as authentic with can be a brief and as an alternative powerful manner to distance your self, experience higher, and benefit a few mind-set.

(iv)   Get Active

Strenuous exercising is a healthful manner to pump your adrenaline and release steam. If you feel stressed, you can want to transport for more enjoyable activities like yoga or walking on your network.

(v)   Do some issue that you enjoy doing

It can be some issue: gardening, portray, playing devices, knitting, analyzing books, playing laptop video video games, or SUDOKU or WORDPRESS.

(c) A grounding Exercise

After triggering a combat or flight response, there can be no way to relax out and 'anticipate in your very very own'. Instead of focusing in your mind, interest on how you feel in your body.

The following floor carrying sports are an clean and speedy manner to interrupt down, loosen up and regain manipulate. It can also need to make a huge difference in only a few minutes. These are a few techniques that one have to need to follow:

Do sitting in a pretty snug feature.

Focus on what you're experiencing to your frame. Feel the level you are sitting on. Feel your toes at the ground. Feel your arms for your lap.

Slowly, take a deep breath and attention to your respiration. Breathe slowly. Hold immediately to the remember amount of 3. Then breathe slowly, preserving it all over again for a consider huge style of three. Keep doing this for several mins.

three.   Tip # 3: Improve your mutual or interpersonal skills

If you've got borderline individual sickness, you may have struggled with maintaining robust, proper relationships with fanatics, co-humans, and buddies. The motive is which you are having issue withdrawing and seeing subjects from wonderful people's perspectives.

You deceive others' mind and emotions, misunderstand how others see you, and forget about how they have got affected your behavior. Identifying your blind spot is step one.

Examine or Check your Assumptions

Stop thru for a projection

(a) Examine your assumptions

When you be afflicted by stress and negatives, as human beings with BPD frequently do, it's miles a good deal much less complex to misinterpret the intentions of others. If you're privy to this phenomenon, take a look at your assumptions.

Remember, you aren't a mind reader! Instead of leaping to the (typically bad) results, bear in mind possibility triggers. For example, let's assume your partner changed into suddenly at the mobile phone with you and now you feel insecure and scared that they have got out of area hobby in you. Before acting on the ones feelings:

Stop with the useful resource of to don't forget precise possibilities

Ask this person to make clean your intentions

Take responsibility for your feature

(i)   Stop through manner of to hold in mind incredible possibilities

Your colleagues may be below pressure at paintings. It can be a disturbing day. Maybe he does now not have enough however. There are severa possibility reasons for this behavior.

(ii)   Ask this person to make clear your intentions

The simplest way to check your assumptions is to invite the opposite man or woman what she or he is wondering or feeling. Double test what they mean through the usage of their phrases or moves.

(b)   Stop through for a projection

To fight projection, you need to learn how to brake - similar to you probably did to stop your emotional conduct. Keep in thoughts your emotions and frame feeling. Note the signs of stress, which include excessive coronary heart price, muscle anxiety, sweating, nausea, or light headedness.

When you feel this manner, you'll be much more likely to assault and say some factor that you will regret later. Hold on and take some deep breaths. Just do ask your self a number of the subsequent questions:

Am I indignant with myself?

Am I ashamed or scared?

Am I involved approximately being dissatisfied?

If the solution is yes, interrupt the conversation. Tell the opportunity man or woman that you are getting emotional and want to count on for a while earlier than discussing topics further.

(c) Take duty for your role

Finally, it's far critical to simply accept the placement you play in your courting. Ask your self how your techniques make a contribution to the problem.

Chapter 2: Bpd & Successful Treatments

Common Therapy

Talk remedy is typically the first choice for remedy (not like some one-of-a-kind ailments in which treatment is most usually accomplished.) Usually, treatment consists of one to two sessions regular with week with a highbrow fitness advertising and marketing and advertising consultant. In order for therapy to be effective, human beings should feel comfortable and assured with their therapist.

It is frequently hard to change feelings of excessive, volatile relationships or emptiness because of the concern that others can also furthermore leave. Research shows that treatment is extra powerful at maximizing paintings and improving social adjustment, further to anger, suicide attempts, and self-damage. People whose symptoms decorate can also moreover however have continual issues, consisting of melancholy, substance abuse, consuming problems, or worrying pressure disease.

However, studies shows that absolutely formed BPD symptoms hardly ever cross back after remission. The results of BPD extend an extended way past that of an individual affected character, which also can harm own family people. Like therapists, cherished ones can battle to answer constructively to the affected character's disturbing moods and needs. For this motive, own family humans can also gain from psychotherapy.

Borderline Personality Disorder (BPD) remedy also can encompass character or group psychotherapy, conducted thru the intellectual health group (CMHT) specialists inside the community. The intention of CMHT is to offer each day assist and remedy. , While making sure that you get as a whole lot freedom as possible. A CMHT may be created:

Social people

Community Mental Health Nurses

Pharmacist

Consultant and Psychologist

Psychologists and Psychologists

Occupational Therapists

Therapies & Treatments

Generally, borderline person illness is essentially dealt with using psychotherapy, however drugs can be protected. If your protection is at hazard, your physician may additionally suggest hospitalization. Treatment will let you to have a take a look at abilities to cope with and cope with your condition.

It is likewise crucial to cope with any other intellectual fitness sickness that is most customarily found with the resource of a person sickness, inclusive of depression or substance abuse. It hurts hundreds to the victimized man or woman. By remedy, you may experience better approximately yourself and stay a strong and worthwhile existence.

There are some beneficial & unusual treatments that allows you to get consolation from Borderline Personality Disorder (BPD). That are given below:

Psychotherapy

Care Program Approach (CPA)

Art treatment

Rethinking of a concept

Medications

1. Psychotherapy

Treatment for BPD commonly consists of some shape of psychotherapy, moreover called psychotherapy. There are many first-rate styles of psychotherapy, however all of those encompass taking the time that will help you advantage a better understanding of what you believe you studied and feel.

In addition to listening and discussing crucial troubles with you, psychologists can propose techniques to remedy troubles and, if crucial, assist you to change your attitudes and behaviors. . Therapy for BPD dreams to assist humans better control their mind and emotions.

Psychological treatment for BPD want to most effective be furnished through a knowledgeable expert. They will commonly be psychologists, psychologists or different professional highbrow fitness experts. The kind of psychotherapy you pick out out can be primarily based on a aggregate of personal desire and specific treatment availability to your neighborhood location.

Depending to your needs and the manner you stay your existence, remedy for BPD can last for a year or greater. Psychotherapy, additionally known as speak remedy. This is a simple remedy approach for borderline character disease. Your therapist can tailor the kind of treatment to superb meet your wishes. The dreams of Psychotherapy are to help you:

Focus in your modern-day functionality to paintings

Learn to control the emotions that you aren't feeling

Reduce your sharpness via helping to have a take a look at feelings in vicinity of appearing on feelings

Work on enhancing relationships with the useful resource of being privy to the emotions of your self and others

Learn about borderline character infection

Long-term outpatient psychotherapy, or "communicate remedy", is an critical a part of any remedy for Borderline Personality Disorder (BPD). Types of psychotherapy that have been tested to be effective embody:

2. Care Program Approach (CPA)

If your signs and symptoms and signs and symptoms are moderate to excessive, you'll be admitted to a remedy software referred to as a Care Program Approach (CPA). CPA is largely a manner to ensure you get the right treatment for your desires. There are four degrees:

Assess your health and social dreams

A Care Plan

Appointment of Care Coordinator

Reviews

(a) Assess your fitness and social wishes

It will allow you to have interaction collectively in conjunction with your very private fitness in addition to the social wishes on your precise fitness plan or method.

(b)   A Care Plan

It is normally designed to Meet Your Health and Social Needs

(c) Appointment of Care Coordinator

Usually your first contact with a social worker or nurse and other CMHT individuals

(d)   Reviews

Where your treatment is reviewed often and any vital modifications to the care plan may be agreed upon

3. Art remedy

Arts or this form of some modern healing strategies may be supplied individually or with a hard and fast as part of the remedy section for humans with BPD. It has a difficult and speedy of treatments. That may additionally moreover encompass:

Art Therapy

Dance Movement Therapy

Drama Therapy

Music Therapy

Arts Therapy objectives to help individuals who discover it hard to specific their mind and feelings orally. Therapy specializes in developing some factor to specific your feelings. These guides are run thru informed therapists, who will let you consider what you have had been given created or whether or not your mind and memories are associated. A route in arts remedy usually involves weekly lessons, which last up to 2 hours.

4. Rethinking of a idea

When BPD turn out to be first defined, the borderline of signs and symptoms and signs and symptoms have turn out to be idea to be what are the two maximum essential varieties of psychological issues: mental issues (signs and symptoms and signs and behavioral tendencies that make the maximum of the truth. Distorted ideology or contact with it's far actually removed (fact) and neurological troubles (characteristic of hysteria or other emotional distress, while the reality-checking and functioning is largely sustained). Since then each the concept of BPD and the diagnostic form of psychiatric troubles have evolved. The Fourth Edition (DSM-IV), a diagnostic and statistical manual for intellectual troubles, removed nerves as a diagnostic elegance, and the authors jogging on the subsequent version recommended modifications that would result in BPD from psychiatric problems together with schizophrenia. Distance to be eliminated. Because BPD is a specifically excessive form of character disorder, affected people often make up a highly huge percentage of patients in intellectual health remedy. It impacts 1% to 2% of US adults, however up to ten% of psychiatric sufferers and 15% to 20% of psychiatric sufferers. An wonderful 69% to eighty% of patients interact in suicidal behavior (which encompass suicide attempts and risk of loss of life) and nine% of patients with BPD die from suicide. For years, formative years tension and abuse - in particular sexual abuse - were taken into consideration as number one chance elements for BPD development. Some research have cautioned that 80 one to 91 sufferers in BPD patients skilled abuse as child abuse. But particular researchers have argued that threat isn't similar to addiction, and that some early studies can be problem to bear in thoughts bias - especially after years of being at a loss for words by way of the usage of patients. The present day thinking about BPD is that it develops because of the interaction of many elements - along side trauma in youngsters who are quickly or genetically inclined. In truth, family and twin research endorse that BPD is sixty nine% inherited, this means that that genes are most susceptible to growing this ailment.

five.   Medications

Medication can not therapy BPD, but it can assist address certainly one of a type situations that frequently accompany BPD, which include despair, fever and tension. People with BPD are recommended to talk to their scientific medical doctor approximately what to expect with every medicine and its facet consequences.

Experts are cut up on whether or now not remedy is useful. Medications can also moreover encompass anti-depressants, antipsychotics or temper stabilizers. Talk to your health practitioner approximately the advantages and difficulty consequences of medication. No drug is presently certified to address BPD.

Although the drug isn't always recommended through the National Institute for Health and Care Excellence (NICE) recommendations, there can be proof that it is able to be useful in some humans with certain issues. If you have got different mental fitness situations, drug treatments are often used collectively with:

Mental stress

Anxiety disease

Bipolar illness

Mode stabilizers or antiseptics are from time to time endorsed to assist with temper swings, alleviate psychotic symptoms and symptoms, or lessen acute conduct. The top notch way to appearance which, if any, medicine options are right for you is to talk on your medical physician or psychologist.

They let you plan an action plan to control the symptoms. Although no pills are currently authorised for borderline personality disorder through the FDA, research has established that some medications alleviate a number of the symptoms of this disease.

Use of medicine may be in particular powerful for BPD whilst used collectively with psychotherapy. In addition to helping with BPD symptoms and signs, medicinal drugs also can help with contemporary intellectual fitness situations, inclusive of tension or despair. Some typically advocated drug treatments for BPD include:

Antidepressants

Antipsychotics

Anxiolytics

Mood Stabilizers

(a) Antidepressants

Antidepressants can assist with emotions of despair.

(b)   Antipsychotics

Antipsychotics are some of the number one tablets used for the remedy of BPD and may be specially useful for symptoms of BPD, which includes tension, angina, and unconscious thoughts. .

(c) Anxiolytics

Anxiolytics, also referred to as anti-tension medicinal tablets. With BPD, anxiety can bypass collectively and some of those capsules are beneficial, despite the fact that some of them are double-edged due to their addictive capability.

(d)   Mood Stabilizers

Mood stabilizers, moreover called anticonvulsants. Mood stabilizers can help with speedy and emotional reactions. Other possible treatments, consisting of omega-three fatty acids, also are being explored. The extremely good proof of the blessings of prescribed drugs in BPD includes 2dgeneration anti-CCT websites and temper stabilizers.

Borderline individual disorder is intensively accountable for very extreme emotional studies. Occasionally, humans with BPD are admitted to a psychiatric hospital for protection.

Patient treatment calls which will live within the health facility in a single day. Another kind of remedy alternative is partial or not unusual hospitalization or day treatment. These are applications which is probably a exceptional deal deeper than conventional outpatient psychotherapy however you do now not must be overnight.

If you'll a catastrophe, or if you have sincerely been hospitalized with inpatients and also you need greater giant care, ensure you do not have a recurrence of the catastrophe. Can be enrolled in a medical institution or day software program application.

Dialectical Behavioral Therapy (DBT)

Dialectical Behavioral Therapy (DBT) is a form of remedy this is specially used to address people with BPD. The time period "dialectical" isn't strictly utilized by any truth seeker who may also moreover furthermore use it. Rather, it refers to a point of view that seeks to reconcile obvious contradictions. Such as accepting the affected person's point of view whilst encouraging change.

Dialectical remedy typically lasts for 3 hundred and sixty five days and consists of each organization and man or woman instructions. During company treatment, sufferers have a look at extra green behaviors and reactions via trouble fixing, mindfulness meditation, muscle relaxation, and breathing schooling training.

During person psychotherapy (regularly supplemented with cellphone schooling), the therapist allows the patient integrate classes from organization durations into their every day lives. Studies executed with the aid of the usage of the use of researchers at

Washington University have concluded that diagnostic behavior is powerful in decreasing suicidal and suicidal ideation, similarly to the substantial form of days spent in psychiatric hospitals.

In one test, there had been a hundred and one ladies with BPD who had attempted suicide as a minimum twice within the past 5 years, with investigators randomly assigned half of to remedy with analgesic treatment and The distinct half of is professional clinicians (who're described as expert and affiliated with valid groups).

Both interventions lasted three hundred and sixty five days. Researchers located that sufferers who underwent dialectical remedy were 1/2 of as possibly when others attempted to devote suicide and were a wonderful deal less in all likelihood to dedicate suicide or to health facility. After 12 months of treatment, sufferers present manner diagnostic remedy were a remarkable deal plenty less probably than those receiving minor care to have interaction in distraction or unique excessive-pace, self-negative behaviors.

Six months after the intervention ended, diagnostic remedy have grow to be an extended manner extra powerful than commonplace remedy. The DBT is primarily based on the idea that 2 vital factors make a contribution to BPD:

You are specifically emotionally willing For example, low degrees of strain make you experience fantastically disturbing.

You grew up in an surroundings wherein your feelings had been rejected with the useful resource of the people around you.

These 2 elements can motive you to be in a vicious circle. You face extreme and demanding feelings, but you still feel accountable and nugatory for feeling those emotions. Because of your upbringing, you believe you studied having those feelings makes you a lousy character. Then these mind reason more worrying emotions.

DBT's intention is to break this cycle through way of introducing 2 key standards.

Verification

Etymology

(a) Verification

Accepting your emotions is correct, actual and applicable

(b)   Etymology

A college of philosophy that publicizes that most subjects in existence can not often be "black or white" and it is important to be open for your mind and mind that contradict your very own.

Moreover

Dialectical Behavior Therapy (DBT) modified into the number one shape of pseudo remedy that is useful for humans with borderline personality sickness (BPD). In this treatment, people discover ways to control conflicts, and learn how to help them cope with sturdy emotions. Meditation is likewise often involved.

DBT specializes in the idea of mentality, or the contemporary emotion. DBT teaches abilities to triumph over immoderate feelings, lessen self-damaging conduct, manipulate misery, and beautify relationships. It seeks to find a balance among accepting and changing attitudes.

Treatment includes in-man or woman treatment training, organization placing abilities schooling, and speak to training as preferred. DBT is the maximum studied remedy for BPD and is one of the first rate.

It (DBT) began out as a way to help manipulate disaster conduct together with suicide behavior or self-harm. This is the maximum commonly advocated remedy for BPD. It works with the concept of mindfulness, or being gift. It helps you to be aware about your emotions, moods and behaviors. You learn capabilities like:

How to cope with terrible feelings

Communicate with feelings efficaciously

DBT consists of organization and character remedy mainly designed to address borderline persona sickness. DBT makes use of a understanding-oriented method to educate you a manner to attend to your emotions, address harm, and improve relationships.

The DBT therapist will use both thoughts to try to make outstanding changes to your conduct. For example, the therapist can renowned (confirm) that feelings of intense melancholy damage you, and that doing so does not make you a frightening and nugatory individual.

However, the therapist will then try to mission the notion that self-harm is the handiest manner to manipulate. The last reason of DBT is to "get rid" of the vicinity, your relationships and your existence from being visible in a completely tight and rigid manner, supporting you've got interplay in dangerous and self-bad behavior.

Usually DBT includes weekly man or woman and enterprise instructions, and if your signs and symptoms and signs worsen you will be given an out-of-hours touch range to call. DBT based mostly on teamwork. You will be anticipated to paintings together with your therapist and specific people in your business enterprise periods.

As a stop stop result, therapists art work together as a crew. DBT has been specially effective in handling ladies with BPD who've a records of self-harming and suicidal behavior. The National Institute for Health and Care Excellence (NICE) has added the primary treatment for these girls.

Schema Focused Therapy

It allow you to select out terrible desires that may result in terrible varieties of lifestyles, which at times can be useful for survival, but as an man or woman you could spend maximum of your lifestyles. The fields are painful. Therapy focuses on assisting you meet your goals in a healthful manner to sell a extraordinary way of life.

Schema Focused Therapy is just like Cognitive Behavioral Therapy, in the manner it rejects awful thoughts approximately itself in exquisite ones. It is likewise a shape of cognitive behavioral therapy for Borderline Personality Disorder (BPD).

Schema-focused remedy runs with the perception that pointless desires from formative years can result in lousy considering the world. This therapy specializes in handling those terrible beliefs and behaviors, and as an opportunity on healthful methods of wondering and coping.

Therapists focus on fostering therapeutic relationships and assisting patients. Guided steering makes use of techniques along facet imagery, affinity training, and characteristic-playing to help address regular reports and disturbing activities. To be powerful, treatment ought to be persevered for at the least years.

In a randomized controlled test which incorporates 86 patients, researchers on the Academic Hospital Maastricht of the Netherlands in comparison schema-targeted therapy to psychotherapy. However, normal, attention on schema have come to be more likely to result in recovery.

Transference-centered psychotherapy

Transference-targeted psychotherapy (TFP) has evolved or designed to help sufferers an superb way to recognize their feelings and interpersonal troubles. It occurs through the mutual courting amongst affected person and therapist. The affected person then makes use of the mastering belief in exclusive situations.

It is likewise referred to as Psycho Dynamic Psychotherapy (PDP). TFP pursuits to help you understand your emotions and interpersonal issues via a growing relationship amongst you and your therapist. Then you follow those insights to the modern-day state of affairs.

Transference Based Psychotherapy (TBP) has been studied for BPD and consistent with those research, analgesic remedy may be genuinely as actual or better. This remedy makes use of the concept of transferring emotions and expectations from the preliminary dating to the winning, that is a key concept in psychodynamic remedy.

Transfer Based Psychotherapy uses the connection among client and therapist to permit therapists to peer how a purchaser relates to others. Then therapists can use this interest to help someone reply extra efficaciously to their one-of-a-type relationships. This therapy is primarily based on the precept, formerly advised with the resource of Dr. Otto Kornberg, a psychiatrist at Cornell University's Well Medical College, that BPD "identifies," failing to mix remarkable and horrible images of itself.

This divergence (seeing humans and situations all the top or horrible or worse) begins in young people however progresses into teens, primary to inner turmoil that aids inside the symptoms of BPD. How clinicians and sufferers paintings together to apprehend the dynamics of psychotherapy and the feelings associated with it, the usage of techniques derived from psychotherapy, and the manner it is able to affect present day functioning.

The motive of remedy is to help patients higher join their mind approximately themselves and different human beings. Patients go to remedy at least twice consistent with week. Cornell researchers randomly assigned 90 sufferers with BPD to as a minimum one-three hundred and sixty five days remedy through switch-primarily based totally certainly remedy, cardiovascular remedy, or adjuvant remedy.

They recommended results for tremendous sixty two who finished remedy for at least nine months. Patients from all 3 corporations have significantly improved melancholy, anxiety, international functioning and network functioning. All 3 interventions worked similarly nicely preferred, however every supplied particular blessings.

Chapter 3: Growing Beyond Borderline Personality Disorder

Borderline Personality Disorder in Adolescents or Youngsters

It is spreading in younger people in addition to kids very extensively. There are some unique factors on the way to describe the importance of Borderline Personality Disorder (BPD) in all ages.

Women and men with vital psychiatric problems, and in particular people with concurrent economic obstacles, may also moreover moreover revel in such immoderate feelings that they devote seriousness. He can stalk, abuse, terrorize, steal, wreck belongings, set fireplace and, even no longer frequently, kill or kill all people. Economic struggles make life more demanding.

And low-earnings people have a great deal much less get right of entry to to powerful psychotherapy. At the equal time, BPD sufferers of any profits level are susceptible to spreading the terrible chaos in the lives of others, first and main in the chaos. Their outbursts of anger and irritation, this is regularly based on misinterpretation of situations, can bring about mistreatment of others, mainly family people.

For girls with extreme BPD, distress, institutionalization or incarceration can also have outcomes. Men who've been diagnosed with a social disorder can, in truth, display a male model of what we name BPD. The unique final consequences for these low-profits "individual sickness" guys is also deeply regrettable.

With little or no hazard of remedy, their way of lifestyles frequently results in incarceration. How unhappy that our society insufficiently is aware of the individual in their problems, whilst it's far urgently had to enhance, teach and psychologically reply with punishment.

Borderline Personality Disorder can be a project for all people. Teen Borderline Personality Disorder (BPD) disrupts adolescent lifestyles. In addition, it furthermore disrupts the circle of relatives. Widespread false impression, a borderline person is adorable to diagnose character disease. Moreover, the identical is real for mother and father and greater youthful humans.

Its victims are greater frequently than not the teenagers or more youthful human beings as they may be slightly near making or preserving new and present relationships. Therefore, its outcomes are generally commonplace in young human beings. There are a few not unusual affects of Borderline Personality Disorder are said under.

Youth can occasionally be afflicted by quite a few moods and irritations. They may sense touchy while omitted. Learning the manner to control emotions is a not unusual part of developing up. For some teens, the ones feelings can be a signal of extra excessive and intense issues.

If your youngster is experiencing severe and common temper swings, immoderate-pace behaviors, self-damage or relationship problems, it can be a mental scenario referred to as Borderline Personality Disorder (BPD). Borderline persona dispositions are complex, stressful, and difficult for cherished ones to apprehend.

This is in particular the case for dad and mom or caregivers who address younger humans who have borderline character illness (BPD). Nevertheless, many specialists say that teens also can have BPD, and adolescent BPD is now recognized because the respectable prognosis.

Many parents have questions about borderline individual. Some humans worry that their youngster is showing symptoms of borderline character ailment (BPD), which include extreme and common mood changes, excessive-pace behaviors, self-harm, or relationship problems. This is a hotly debated question.

Many experts argue that technically a person under the age of 18 ought to now not be identified with a borderline persona; his individual has now not but been absolutely fashioned. In the present day model of the Diagnostic and Statistical Manual of Mental Disorders (DSM-five), but, there may be a provision that lets in the analysis of borderline man or woman earlier than the age of 18.

Borderline Personality Disorder (BPD) is a commonplace and excessive mental sickness associated with severe purposeful impairment and high charges of suicide. BPD is typically related to better mental and character issues, greater burden on circle of relatives and caregivers, permanent use of assets, and better treatment prices. BPD has been a debatable analysis in younger humans, however is no longer valid. Recent evidence indicates that BPD is as reliable and legitimate in young adults as it is in adults and that teens with BPD may additionally gain from early intervention.

As a end quit result, adolescent BPD is now recognized in mental score structures and restoration hints. To enhance the properly-being and extended-term assessment of those human beings, BPD analysis and remedy need to be considered a part of normal exercise in adolescent highbrow fitness.

Symptoms

Although the signs of BPD as listed within the legitimate DSM-five diagnostic standards aren't any individual of a kind for teens and adults, some experts have recommended that there are variations inside the signs of teenager BPD as well. Symptoms, together with instability in a relationship, sturdy thoughts-set, continual vacancy, and risky emotions of self, may appear otherwise among kids.

There are powerful healing alternatives for recovery teenager borderline persona disorder. Further, modern-day research demonstrates this fact. As a forestall result, maximum humans get better over the years with borderline persona sickness. Effective Borderline Personality Disorder Treatment combines clinical perspectives and holistic techniques. In addition, such remedy can help to strengthen BPD conduct and reduce every day emotional stressful situations.

In maximum young people, BPD may be treated early and correctly. Also, in maximum times, early treatment for teenager borderline character infection is usually recommended. Therefore, such early treatment effects in better prolonged-term results.

Difficulty coping with mind and emotions

Dangerous and horrifying behaviors

Difficulties in relationships

(a) Difficulty handling mind and feelings

In this situation, one has to stand awful effects in their low manage on their thoughts & emotions. This detail influences hundreds to a person with a view to acquire their private life's dreams. Such parents have low self-control and horrible emotional common sense. Consequently, they fails to get a pleasing existence. Some of the following awful outcomes of Borderline Personality Disorder are as follow:

Frequent dramatic modes swirl

Episodes of anger

Feeling "empty" or "apathetic"

Repeated adjustments to the photo itself

Suicidal thoughts

(b)   Dangerous and provoking behaviors

Sometimes, Borderline Personality Disorder lefts deep impact on the psychy and the behaviors of someone's private lifestyles. In the stop give up result, one becomes dissatisfied which will advantage unique or regular behaviors. The essential reason of this conduct is to drop or loss strength of mind and plenty much less motion on behaviors.

Consequently, sufferers get dangerous, extraordinary and provoking behaviors. That harm lots to them and located a deep and worrying impact to their lives. Some of the primary problems confronted via way of the patients are as check:

Self-damage (which includes slicing or burning yourself)

Suicide behavior

Unsafe sexual encounters

Illegal drug use

(c) Difficulties in Relationships

Relationships are the maximum crucial and essential a part of a person's each day primarily based life. They have a sizeable impact in surely each person's life. Either he / she is youngster or antique. It is the splendor of nature which wants to be completed via many elements.

We are all engaged inside the net of relationships. Their lifestyles and significance performs an crucial role in our lives. We get concerned on getting breakups in addition to being satisfied on getting new ones to our lives. Once we're engaged in a current day relation, we get proper feelings and personifications. Some of the main defects on can face in this case are as look at:

Invalid range

Serious and risky relationships

Great efforts to keep away from being rejected or abandoned

Feeling misunderstood

Causes of BPD

Many youths are capable of provide an motive for them without borderline individual illness. It must be cited. Nevertheless, it is a red flag to answer certain to those questions. Such responses propose that proactive measures want to be taken in the direction of professional assessment.

The motives for the borderline character illness are not completely understood. It is, of direction, the ultimate mixture of environmental and genetic elements. Possible BPD reasons include:

Genetic Factors

Neurological Factors

Traumatic History

(a) Genetic Factors

No unique BPD gene has been recognized to this point. Nevertheless, education in twins shows a strong inherent link. Therefore, scientists concluded that genetics play a role inside the impairment of personality throughout borders. BPD genetic studies are pushing.

However, those preliminary effects are searching earlier to duplication. Larger pattern sizes and extra correct strategies are desired. Nevertheless, consistent with the most current-day clinical version, the frontiers are focused in households. Genetic strain is the key to such cognizance problems.

(b)   Neurological Factors

BPD sufferers lack the neurological capability needed to prevent negative feelings. In this manner, the a part of the mind that controls the emotions and controls the continuity. Therefore, such loss offers rise to behavioral troubles and character problems.

Studies display the danger of abnormalities inside the shape of the thoughts. About 60% of borderline man or woman sickness is at danger. In addition, the neurological reaction to continual stress is a likely motive. Chronic pressure exposure can possibly alternate the metabolism and structure of the mind. Such adjustments may also moreover restrict the mind's competencies.

It can limit the processing and integration of emotions and mind. This finding illustrates the significance of early intervention. Indeed, early intervention can relieve chronic stress. Such early intervention minimizes nerve harm and improves rehabilitation effects.

(c) Traumatic History

Often, this trauma includes bodily abuse, excessive strain, and / or abandonment. However, the trauma of the abuse is outdoor the circle of relatives unit. Many humans record borderline disturbing activities with Borderline Personality Disorder. In fact, maximum rise up for the duration of children.

Unstable relationships and early exposure to enemy conflicts are also viable factors. Additionally, most human beings with a records of annoying life sports activities do no longer have borderline character disease. Therefore, it is crucial to make such differences.

When taken together, the above reasons spotlight the need for early intervention. In truth, early interventions can lessen the capacity for damage. With more youthful human beings, early intervention is important.

Impacts of Borderline Personality Disorder

Borderline Personality Disorder (BPD) is a mental condition characterized by means of the use of risky relationships, worry of being deserted, issues in emotion control, emotions of vacancy, chronic dysphoria or melancholy, as well as speedy and Identifies endangered behaviors.

Paranoid Editions and disassociated states are also a brief characteristic of the syndrome. In addition, many patients with BPD time and again show off self-harming or suicidal conduct. BPD has a bent of approximately 6% for the duration of life. This could be very not unusual in the clinical putting, consequently making BPD quite appropriate for healthcare providers and the overall public.

BPD's ontological models recommend that the development of 'distrustful inner operating fashions' primarily based totally on risky attachments has the functionality to render others untrustworthy and rejected. Factors that cause this development encompass children trauma which encompass emotional neglect approximately or bodily and sexual abuse, despite the fact that linking BPD to traumatic sports activities is just one greater example.

The contribution of genetics to BPD is unsure, however the inheritance of BPD appears to be big. The preliminary distress revel in, specifically the associated data, the emotional irritability of the trauma or the abuser, provides the individual's expectations regarding the supply of destiny sources, together with the reliability and trustworthiness of others in interpersonal relationships.

BPD is mostly a intellectual scenario of different psychiatric problems (formerly concept to be axis I troubles in step with DSM-IV), the maximum important being despair, special persona issues, and bipolar ailment (BD) with syndrome overlap or comorbidity, interest deficit / hyperactivity ailment (ADHD) and publish-stressful stress illness (PTSD).

In preserving with traditional scientific ideas, many students view BPD as a scientific syndrome with identifiable cerebral lesions or defects, normally affecting the fronto-limbic connectivity, which results in sufferers' emotional instability, not able to coping with mutual misery.

However, such perspectives are contradictory; those observations suggest that the mutual problems of human beings with BPD are in massive element absent from emotionally tough conditions, and over the years many patients Self-dealing and contradictions suffer a substantial discount, despite the fact that entire rehabilitation is uncommon and mutual. Difficulties and emotional instability are greater not unusual.

In truth, maximum intellectual conditions get worse with growing age, so why have to BPD be an exception as well? Another counter-intuitive problem with BPD is that threat taking behaviors and depressions percentage the equal situation below which humans with melancholy are usually at danger, in region of BPD.

Finally, controversies upward push up approximately the presence of BPD and intercourse versions in scientific presentation, maximum of which stay unresolved, in all likelihood due to ideological range. In view of these conceptual contradictions, the winning article tries to shed a terrific mild on BPD. It has been cautioned that a few abilties of BPD can be better understood within the frame of reference, considering environmental insights into the behavior.

Accordingly, specific understandings, emotions and behaviors of BPD can be full-size and inclusive, every now and then even logical, whilst imagining a global this is risky and unpredictable, in which one is "sharp and indignant." .Have a 'way of lifestyles suitable' look. Such a view does not imply that BPD is consistent with second.

Instead, it's miles advised that character signs and symptoms and signs and symptoms associated with BPD can be synchronized meaningfully from a life-facts mindset, and that BPD subscales or 'dilute' phenotypes are real. Can be paid productively (which means being biologically), despite the fact that probable at the price of nicely-being and intellectual fitness.

In terms of medical implications, it is claimed that a behavioral ecological method also can be an extended way from the symptoms and signs and symptoms and signs (for instance; "ease") of focusing in terms of mental healing capabilities, aimed closer to the existence of an character. Is to reject the records method as an lousy lot as possible. Practical strategies to include and beautify their recognition of kids tales with conducting current biosocial desires.

Risk elements for borderline individual ailment in teens are very similar to hazard elements in adults. In truth, many environmental threat factors for BPD upward push up in early life. For example, parental separation or disappearance, alongside side youth abuse and neglect, is related to borderline persona in adults and young people.

Research has moreover proven that children whose dad and mom have a excessive highbrow fitness circumstance (which consist of despair, substance abuse or social man or woman) are also at greater hazard for BPD. In addition, there are probably natural hazard elements for BPD, which includes the genetic element of an inherited ailment. There are some excessive impacts of Borderline Personality Disorder. That impacts the human nature in addition to its neurons. Some of them are as have a look at:

Suicide due to BPD

Misdiagnosis

Misdiagnosed Disorders

(a) Suicide due to BPD

When it consists of kids with BPD, the chance of self-harm and suicide can not be decreased. In addition, borderline personality sickness consists of suicide or self-harming behavior among its diagnostic requirements.

Further, it is a single character sickness that consists of such standards. 70% of human beings with borderline character sickness will as a minimum strive suicide. Worse, close to 10% of people with BPD will commit suicide. As a quit cease result, this mortality rate is to 3 times better than in schizophrenia.

In truth, this is the outstanding fee of suicide in highbrow fitness troubles. Moreover, the suicide charge of BPD is 50 instances better in the fashionable populace of the united states. Finally, it's miles vital to make sure the protection of the surroundings for extra younger humans with BPD. Therefore, proscribing access to lethal property is an powerful shape of suicide prevention.

(b)   Misdiagnosis

Borderline personality sickness may be tough to diagnose. In this manner, teenager borderline persona illness is frequently misdiagnosed. In addition, evaluation of borderline individual illness has been tough from the start. This trouble is contemplated in its name.

In 1938, psychologist Adolf Stern coined the term "borderline." It first explained maximum of the signs. They at the moment are a part of the Borderline Personality Disorder diagnostic necessities. Regions face borderline person ailment. In this manner, they exploded amongst neurosis and psychosis. In fact, the misdiagnosis records of BPD are incredible. In one have a look at, forty% of human beings were misdiagnosed as borderline man or woman contamination. He became diagnosed with bipolar ailment.

(c) Misdiagnosed Disorders

Misdiagnosis gives the capacity for anxiety. They must be evaluated thru skilled experts. They want a definitive compare via an occupational therapist. This prognosis is critical. Here are a number of the problems which can be typically misdiagnosed in BPD patients:

Bipolar Disorder

Depression

Teen Anxiety

Adolescent substance Abuse

Trauma

(i)   Bipolar Disorder

The emotional instability of BPD seems like a bipolar sickness. There can be mistakes in cycling among mania and unhappiness.

(ii)   Depression

BPD poor temper changes were misidentified as signs of adolescent despair.

(iii)   Teen Anxiety

A Great Trouble Born With Fear of Abandonment. This can be a mistake for adolescent anxiety.

(iv)   Adolescent substance abuse

Drug or alcohol abuse is a BPD coping mechanism. Abuse of such materials is frequently regular. It is regularly fallacious for teenage substance abuse.

(v)   Trauma

It is proper that trauma often impacts BPD within the young adults. But the borderline personality disorder is from time to time disregarded. Instead, a assessment of youngsters trauma or PTSD (Post Traumatic Stress Disorder) is given.

Important topics you may understand

"Borderline Personality Disorder (BPD) is a mental infection characterised with the beneficial resource of an ongoing sample of diverse moods, self-expression, and behaviors." As a cease result, BPD sufferers regularly act prejudiced, have tumultuous relationships, and experience episodes of anger, disappointment, and tension.

But for individuals who have not weighed in on BPD themselves or their loved ones, this explanation won't make a superb deal feel to you. There are some vital detail you need to realise approximately Borderline Personality Disorder (BPD). Some of them are given under:

Feeling too much

Unapproachable Love

To be Limited

Emptiness

Scaring your self

Traumas & Traumatic History

Love: The Essence of lifestyles

(i)   Feeling an excessive amount of

People with BPD are emotionally touchy at begin. This tremendous sensitivity lets in humans with BPD to experience emotions at a far higher and greater excessive degree than normal. Offers.

This is specifically tough in demanding situations even as handling our inherent emotional dysregulation problems will become more tough. In truth, we do now not advise to act on our feelings so frequently.

(ii)   Unapproachable Love

Because of this, our love for you could attain heights you've got got in no manner skilled. When we fall for something or some aspect, we get difficult. The emotional element of our mind is the component that regularly leaves us in the back of without our permission our It will become the focus of our interest.

Relationships with us can be more than faith, a concept of affection that surrounds you with every reward and encouragement you offer. We need you to be successful and be an amazing character that we think about and sense you belong to, and we ought to do some thing we need to do to reveal that.

(iii)   To be Limited

Still, we're able to sometimes be bloodless and a long way flung. However, loads of a few element may be horrible for you, even love. Sometimes our brains pressure us to question our relationships.

Do they love us sufficient?

Do they virtually recognize that how plenty we experience for them?

If they do no longer, are we able to appearance silly and hurt all over again? This is on the equal time as the harmful anti-depressant method is located. Even people who experience too much cannot teach themselves to sense some factor. People with

BPD are very touchy and could do some thing they might to save you this sense of proper or perceived abandonment.

(iv)   Emptiness

These feelings regularly become overwhelming. People with BPD are identified to be very effective. However, the muse reason is likewise important. The emotions of emptiness is likewise one of the most commonplace effect of Borderline Personality Disorder.

This isn't always your common 10 minutes of boredom due to the fact you experience lazy or tired. No, it's far a everlasting feel of natural location that is hungry for a experience of which means that, of any direction, thru the reputedly inaccessible entrances of your mind. We want to do a little component to give up it. Unfortunately, this often includes affective, careless, and self-unfavourable behaviors.

(v)   Scaring yourself

Sometimes we scare ourselves (too much). In fact, this acute form of mental contamination have become taken into consideration on the border line among psychosis and neurosis, it is why it's miles now termed as "borderline character disorder."

While BPD has an emphasis on emotional disorder, plenty people moreover enjoy debilitating styles of psychosis, which consist of confusion and overwhelming discrimination. In truth, isolation is one of the competencies of BPD.

Imagine being crushed with the aid of manner of feelings and out of doors motivations that you can not enjoy grounded on your personal international - as in case you had been saved from fact and now from an external issue of view to keep away from traumatic conditions.

(vi)   Traumas & Traumatic History

The traumas of our beyond play a good deal extra than we realize. Environmental outcomes make a contribution to the development of BPD. Such outcomes consist of kids overlook, abuse, misery and aggravation with a family member suffering from immoderate highbrow contamination.

When demanding activities rise up in some unspecified time in the destiny of early formative years, wholesome development may be solid and may purpose issues later in life. It also can be the give up result of black-and-white wondering, lack of balance of the item, and preserving little one-like behaviors collectively with emotional contradictions.

We won't apprehend (or need to understand) the consequences of our childhood in our person lives, but are able to heal those open wounds and try and turn out to be aware about their function in our BPD.

Chapter 4: What Is Borderline Personality Disorder (Bdp)

A borderline personality sickness is some of the most outstanding of the ten DSM IV-TR individual troubles. "Personality contamination" is defined as a cluster of an person's prolonged-popularity, ingrained inclinations. Such developments are usually observable through early adulthood, puberty, or maybe in advance, and result in maladaptive, unfavourable styles of conduct, notion and connection to others. The diagnoses of person problems are separated via way of manner of placement at a separate magnificence (Axis II) from maximum distinct psychiatric ailments. Other psychiatric illnesses, which incorporates melancholy, schizophrenia, drug abuse, and consuming issues are described in Axis I. While Axis 2 is a long term continual behavioral disease, Axis I troubles are historically seen as time-limited, more natural and extra susceptible to medicine. Axis I signs and symptoms generally recede in order that humans can cross again to their "herbal" position among disorder exacerbations. Persons with recognized person problems typically specific dysfunctional traits even after the acute trouble has been solved. Cure usually takes a long term because it entails converting behavior patterns substantially. Personality troubles, mainly BPD, have examined to reason greater severe daily useful impairment than some of Axis I issues, together with fundamental despair.

BPD stocks many signs, especially histrionic, narcissistic, schizotypal, antisocial, and primarily based totally man or woman problems of different person dysfunctions. However, BPD distinguishes itself from other distortions in its constellation of vehicle-destruction, continual feelings of vacuity and decided fears of abandonment.

BPD's important tendencies are impulsiveness and agitation in assessment, self-photograph and moods. These behavioral patterns are commonplace, generally beginning in youth and persisting for extended intervals of time. The analysis is primarily based mostly on the following nine requirements consistent with the DSM-IV-TR (and is usually normal in the global). An man or woman must show 5 of those 9 signs and symptoms to be diagnosed with BPD.

Criteria for BPD

1.   Always attempts to keep away from actual or perceived abandonment

2.   A sample of unstable and immoderate interpersonal relations that change among idealization and devaluation extremes

3.   Disruption of identification: Markedly and continuously volatile self-picture or experience of self

four.   Series of impulsion in at least viable self-destructive areas (e.G., spending, age, misuse of medication, ruddy the usage of, binge ingesting)

5. Recurrent conduct, actions, threats, or self-mutilation

6. Affective (temper) instability and marked environmental reactivity (e.G. Severe episodic melancholy, irritability or anxiety everyday for multiple hours and seldom a number of days)

7. Chronic emptiness feelings

8. Inappropriate, severe anger or problems controlling frustration (e.G. Repeated temperature changes, immoderate rage, repetitive bodily battles)

nine. Transient anxiety or immoderate dissociative symptoms (emotions of unreality)

It may be seen from a better have a look at those conditions in later chapters, the modern-day DSM-IV-TR simply underlines mild symptom description revisions. Then, the most important exchange is the appearance of the 9th criterion that accepts occasional quick psychotic episodes. This constellation of nine signs and symptoms and signs and symptoms can be divided into 4 important regions of treatment:

1. Instability in temper (requirements 1, 6, 7 and eight)

2. Uncontrolled behaviors and Impulsivity (necessities 4 and 5)

three. Psychopathological interpersonal association (necessities 2 and 3)

four. Thought and belief distortions (Criterion 9)

Changes in mood and impulsiveness are the most vital factors in suicide risk. These defining criteria have been grouped in three categories for category via manner of a collaborative, longitudinal check finished by way of researchers during the usa of a. Since interviewing and classifying loads of BPD patients, the researchers reestablished the validity of the BPD-defining DSM variables. The three factors that have been superior are disturbed relationships, out of manage behavior and irregularities in the mood.

Disturbed relationships encompass self-associated and different troubles. Obviously, identity disruption can cause relationship issues. When identification loss of self assurance persists, vacancy and meaninglessness frequently growth. Dissociation from truth while the texture of self disappears altogether.

Uncontrolled behaviour consists of disruptive electricity and self-terrible behaviour. The final standards encompass temper irregularity. Instability of the temper moreover outcomes in frustration and rage. These immoderate emotions alienate others and depart the person on my own and deserted.

These DSM requirements outline a selected BPD definition paradigm; i.E., both someone has it (as a minimum 5 of the BPD requirements are protected) or does now not (with 4 or fewer signs and signs). This conceptualization lets in goal determinants to be measured. All nine criteria, however, are further contributive, allowing the plain paradox that someone with the supposedly lasting diagnosis of BPD may also want to be' healed' of the disease via way of overcoming even one defining criterion. In assessment, a few authors argued that person issues which may be lasting inclinations need to be measurably defined. This version indicates that character levels paintings, similar to the stages or fees of dependancy. Some authors argue that the state of affairs have to be recognized in spectrum with the resource of the severity of the signs and symptoms and signs and symptoms and signs and by way of way of weighting different parameters and records records proportionately in preference to assuming that the individual is or does not have limits. Consider, for example, that the self-control of male or female is specific and objectively determined with the useful resource of several requirements. Alternatively, guys's or girls's designations are dimensional, non-public, cultural and other a lot less intention problems. Proposals for the destiny DSM-V encompass a redefining of individual troubles (Axis II) the use of length fashions.

HISTORY OF BDP

In the united states, the phrase "borderline" grow to be first used in 1938. Early psychologists used this term to explain patients who had been taken into consideration to be on the "line" of illnesses, regularly depression and neurosis. Those with neurosis had been concept to be treatable on the time, whilst human beings with psychoses have been taken into consideration untreatable.

A deeper expertise of the borderline persona disorder then began to emerge in the Seventies. Individuals with BPD were defined as being very emotional, inclined, complex, liable to suicide and having an erratic number one degree of functioning.

Eventually, a pattern of signs and signs and signs to pick out people with borderline persona ailment began to emerge. These included:

Unstable self-photograph

Fear of abandonment

Rapid transition from self guarantee to normal despair

Strong tendency for suicide and self-damage

Rapid and inconsistent mood swing

In 1980, Borderline Personality Disorder (BPD) have come to be a recognized personality ailment in DSM III or Diagnostic and Statistical Manual Mental Disorders III.

SOME MYTHS ABOUT BPD

BPD is a intellectual contamination often misunderstood through the general population or even a few fitness care practitioners. BPD is also known as BPD. It is likewise a sickness that may have a negative impact on the lives of others. There are many myths approximately BPD because of the ones issues. It is so vital to recognize the reality about the sickness if you or someone you recognize is BPD an awesome manner to start healing. Below are a number of the maximum common BPD myths.

Myth 1: Untreatable Borderline Personality Disorder

This is absolutely faux; BPD can be treated. Do no longer let this myth frighten you from remedy if you assume you've got BPD, or make you experience helpless.

A analysis does no longer endorse you may experience BPD symptoms and signs and symptoms all the time. Hard artwork and efficient remedy can reduce BPD symptoms significantly and could allow you to to live a everyday lifestyles.

Even without remedy, signs and signs and symptoms of the disease will ebb and float over time; a few people with BPD can function extra correctly than others.

Myth 2: All People with BPD Are Victims Of Childhood Abuse

All too often people of tremendous intentions who do no longer apprehend BPD bear in mind it's miles due to youth abuse. This can trade how human beings engage with you or speak with you when you have BPD, which may be traumatic if you have no abuse. It may additionally additionally enjoy love it is not understood or awesome to your very own enjoy. While a few people who have BPD were abused, this is not proper for all sufferers with BPD and should be visible with a greater open thoughts.

Till this present minute, there may be no appeared purpose of BPD. The reason is generally seemed rather than being related to anyone reason as a combination of natural and environmental factors.

Myth 3: Adults and Children Cannot Be Diagnosed with Bipolar Personality Disorder

With BPD, kids and kids can not be diagnosed with borderline person troubles. However, due to the usually often happening perception that man or woman remains developed sooner or later of childhood, it modified into controversial to diagnose youngsters or teenagers with BPD.

The fifth edition of the Diagnostic Statistical Manual (DSM-V) devices out easy necessities for the evaluation of BPD. You have to be careful to use whilst developing a analysis, in particular for BPD, because the symptoms often replicate brand new teenage behaviour. A professional BPD therapist can help to differentiate the difference. Early analysis can assist to make certain that an person receives the technique essential to start restoration.

Myth 4: Bipolar Personality Disorder Is A Variation Of Bipolar Disorder

Bipolar persona illness and bipolar sickness are completely one-of-a-kind. While bipolar and BPD signs and symptoms may also seem pretty comparable, they'll be incredible illnesses.

Since even healthcare providers are blind to BPD, human beings with bipolar ailment are frequently misdiagnosed and pressured. It is as nicely important to look at that tablets for the treatment of bipolar illness regularly do no longer artwork for BPD sufferers, consequently it is crucial that a BPD-based absolutely therapist collect a suitable prognosis and remedy plan.

Myth 5: BPD Is Found Only In Women

BPD is positioned in each sexes, although it is real that girls are identified with BPD extra regularly than men.

However, this doesn't in all manner advise girls are more likely to broaden BPD. It may moreover propose that men' symptoms are related to unique illnesses, on the aspect of post-traumatic stress disease or depression, extra incorrectly. The characteristics of BPD are instability and awful pulse manipulate, that may in addition have an effect on every sexes.

Myth 6: If You Know Someone With BPD, You Know Them In All Way

Everyone is unique, and having BPD does no longer change that. You recognise anybody.

The DSM-V present day for intellectual fitness calls for tremendous criteria for the evaluation of BPD. The criterion covers character impairment and interpersonal relationships. The way those impairments are tested in every person is fantastic.

Moreover, now not everyone revel in positive signs and symptoms in the same manner. The trouble of a person with relationships may be awesome from yours. Each person revel in BPD in very great techniques:

Problems In Diagnosis: Related and Coexisting Illnesses

Researches within the final decade have showed that BPD is lots extra regularly than modified into formerly notion associated with different psychiatric illnesses. Unlike the "Farmer inside the Dell" cheese, BPD seldom stands by myself. Some of the defining symptoms and signs and symptoms and signs and symptoms are same to special disease standards. For instance, as with borderlines, many humans residing with ADHD show impatience, Impulsivity, anger pace, broken relationships, negative arrogance and commonplace drug abuse. Antisocial character sickness is characterized thru impulsiveness and outbursts of anger. Depression is the most commonplace "fellow vacationer" with BPD. More than ninety five% of BPD sufferers furthermore satisfy this ailment necessities. Nearly 90 percentage of frontiers furthermore meet standards for anxiety, specially publish-annoying strain ailment, and panic and social anxiety disease. Although both genders enjoy despair and anxiety in addition, drug abuse and sociopaths are visible considerably extra regularly on male borders, at the identical time as eating issues and positioned up-traumatic pressure problems are correlated with girls's borders extra frequently. All the ones ailments are located in borderline areas an entire lot extra often than with one-of-a-kind persona issues.

Because borders usually have numerous afflictions, the clinician want to first deal with the signs and symptoms which can be the maximum disabled. And she ought to juggle the outcomes on accompanying issues of remedy. Many borderlines have accompanying ADHD signs and signs, as an example. With the borderline signs and symptoms of rage and temper change end up worse at the equal time as she initiates remedy for the lousy awareness and distractibility of stimulant medicine? Conversely, will she be capable of keep interest accurately at the way to advantage from remedy if she engages the patient in significant psychotherapy? To make certain thorough and balanced remedy, accurate diagnosis of all issues is important.

BPD can also imitate distinct sicknesses. Mood adjustments may be identified as bipolar sickness incorrectly. Temporary psychosis may furthermore imitate schizophrenia. When an related ailment inclusive of depression or alcoholism is high-quality, the big underlying BPD may be camouflaged. Although BPD may additionally moreover accompany exclusive diseases, distinguishing it from special troubles is essential. Borderline depression and mood swings are commonly associated with situational situations and might therefore exchange interior hours. Major depressive and bipolar problems final for days or longer and won't have any interplay with occasions within the lifestyles of someone. Furthermore, a person with a ailment normally works nicely among episodes, on the equal time as the borderline can hold to behavior itself in negative behaviour. Temporary pressure-related borderline psychosis may furthermore appear acutely like paranoid schizophrenia. However, psychosis in BPD is brief-lived and might sometimes dissolve inside hours. Schizophrenic psychotic sickness is normally persistent and plenty less related to outside stressors. While borderlines furthermore recover from traumas, put up-worrying stress ailment (PTSD) is characterised via specific vital crises reactions. Recurring intrusive questioning at the occasion, keeping off related web web websites or sports activities sports, and hyper-vigilance with over-starting responses are not regular of BPD. Physiological versions advocate that BPD sufferers are extra attentive to abandonment troubles, on the identical time as PTSD patients have a extra immoderate response to trauma-emphasizing suggests.

Diagnostic Bias

BPD is regularly misdiagnosed and underdiagnosed irrespective of its frequency. Primary care physicians, who're normally the first to be handled for psychiatric issues, can diagnose and treat BPD with precision much less than half of of the time.

Coexisting diseases may additionally lead in numerous strategies to the underneath-evaluation of BPD. Many clinicians forget about the analysis of Axis II at the same time as every exceptional sickness is number one, focusing on the treatment of Axis 1 (usually less complicated to address, due to the fact its reputation is on medication in place of on complicated big psychotherapy). In addition, managed care companies occasionally discourage ongoing treatment for person problems, as such sufferers commonly want greater in depth–and additional steeply-priced–lengthy-time period treatment. Many insurance businesses have to truely deny repayment for BPD, announcing that the favored expensive care isn't always part of the insurance. Paradoxically, some medical case managers deny certification on the wrong assumption that proscribing patients never get better, that care does not decorate, and that therapy is, consequently, seeking to waste sources. Many docs, consequently, avoid the borderline label to limit troubles with controlled care businesses.

Finally, due to its stigma within the career, many clinicians are reluctant to diagnose BPD. Borderline patients are the maximum anxious among many practitioners. They have a very stressful reputation with not unusual mobile cellphone calls and interest agitation. They are the maximum arguable psychiatric community. When they'll be dissatisfied, their anger is difficult to tolerate. Constant suicide threats may be hard to manipulate. The treatment requires a bargain patience or maybe greater time, frequently no longer well identified or reimbursed in extremely-modern weather. So many BPD identified patients can't method trained physicians who are inclined to accept them in care.

Roots of BPD

Several techniques had been employed to research the reasons and roots of BPD. Family studies have confirmed that most borderlines have skilled crucial developmental disturbances, indicating environmental reasons.

Recent neurological and genetic researches have theorized that organic foundations can be heritable. An essential borderline subgroup has a statistics of perinatal or received mind harm.

A new studies line that blends genetic/natural vulnerabilities with environmental traumas to create minimum coping mechanisms. A version shows that hereditary (called temperament) dispositions have interaction with developmental (man or woman) values to generate character. So temperament + character=individual. Specific temperaments also may be discerned and associated with biologic imbalances and sensitivities. Temperament fashions increase early in lifestyles and are appeared as instinctual or regular. Character styles steadily come into being and culminate in maturity.

Anatomical and Biological Correlates

Some of the most interesting new studies of BPD research use present day fitness techniques to research the workings of the mind, including chemical exchange control and the identification of anatomic changes. Some studies have confirmed that excessive neurotransmitter serotonin degrees (a chemical that has a nerve conductivity all spherical the body however specifically within the thoughts) may moreover additionally cause an increase in BPD impulsivity and aggression. Interestingly, such sensitivity is visible extra regularly in girls, who account for 75% of borders. One take a look at used positron emission tomography (PET) scanning in guys's and women's BPD's brains to reveal lower degrees of serotonin hobby that correlated with extended Impulsivity. Certain neurotransmitters together with dopamine and GABA moreover can be concerned in the law of impulsive aggression. The acetylcholine and norepinephrine neurotransmitters are related to mood modulation. Medicines to manipulate those imbalances in neurotransmitters have been tested to lessen borderline signs and symptoms.

Many scientists have studied the link among BPD and autoimmune issues, where the frame reacts allergically and develops antibodies within the path of its very non-public organs. Rheumatoid arthritis, for instance, is associated with an enormously immoderate prevalence of BPD. One take a look at modified into completed on a woman with fluctuating BPD symptoms and signs over 9 months, at the same time as her antithyroid antibodies had been measured. Such researchers located drastically decrease antibody prices throughout times on the identical time as their despair and paranoia had been low, and better when their signs and symptoms extended. This finding suggests that autoimmune infection also can exacerbate or vice versa BPD signs and signs.

Scientists who have a check BPD neurology have targeted on part of the thoughts known as the limbic gadget. The mind element influences reminiscence, reading, emotional situations (as an instance, anxiety), and behavior (particularly aggressive and sexual).

Borderline EEG analyzes have confirmed disease in this a part of the brain. One research used magnetic resonance imaging in borderline women with a trauma records to test improvements in limbic tool period. Such authors have shown appreciably decreased amount on this mind place's hippocampus and amygdala regions. This link amongst past physical or emotional traumas and subsequent changes in thoughts extent related to frontier disorder will increase the threat for infant abuse to affect thoughts function, resulting in borderline movements. The direction of the business enterprise turned into now not sincerely seen. Another rationalization can be that BPD causes (in desire to inflicting) adjustments in the volume of the thoughts which might be extraordinary fortuitously associated with the beyond trauma.

Environmental and Genetic Roots

In cutting-edge years, genetic and environmental Roots genome paintings has exploded. Gene mapping, cloning ability and stem cell production have created new limits of medical disorder facts and care. Certain BPD researchers have attempted to determine that precise genes may be responsible for precise borderline behavior sorts. Identity instability, trade of temper and competitive impulsiveness, for instance, have strong inherited additives. Another behaviour sometimes displayed within the absence of limits, a search of delight— which corresponds to the choice for ardour and every so often to the hazard of being bored — is also correlated with distinctive BPD parameters, together with impulsiveness and violence. The Interesting detail is that a few researches have correlated this observable conduct with chemical dysregulation of the device of serotonin neurotransmitters and extraordinary studies on a high fine human chromosome with a gene loci concerning a dopamine neurotransmitter. Though real, the ones studies recommend links among biology, inner chemical equilibrium and in the long run behaviour.

Family studies have confirmed that first-grade borderline family are 5 times much more likely to diagnose the BPD as the public. Borderline family individuals also are much more likely to be diagnosed with related illnesses, in particular with drug abuse, affective issues and delinquent individual disease. During one's life, sure genes were affected, in a way, "on and stale," thru the utilization of factors together with parental repute. Positive parenting can effect genetic predisposition and subsequent biochemical equilibrium in animal and human studies that exams maternal care. A man or woman can also moreover for this reason be born with indigenous vulnerabilities to impaired mind circuitry to modulate moods and Impulsivity, but environmental factors can also effect gene expression to determine whether or not or no longer or not the character has any or all ability restrained signs.

Chapter 5: Causes Of Borderline Personality Disorder: Genetic And Environmental Causes

The motives for this are a complex combination of genetic makeup, the way wherein genes are expressed and interpreted and harnessed below pressure, environmental situations (even circle of relatives interactions), mind maturation, intellectual charter and development

People often ask if there may be a mind test, blood test, or genetic test to grow to be aware of BPD. Then, there may be no such take a look at right now; but, mind scans and extraordinary checks can be used in tandem with measurable moves whilst diagnosing BPD. It isn't going that BPD is a unmarried cause, however is as an alternative a stop result of the accumulation of threat elements in a prone individual.

 I will make clean this by pointing to specific research in every region. While adults have been involved in maximum of this take a look at, masses of them advocate traumas or distinct reasons in early life or youth.

BRAIN STRUCTURE AND BPD

When we observed James as a six-month-vintage, the adoption company suggested us that he had a skull fracture, however he had no neurological problems. "What did he do? But he is momentous, irritated and manipulative now. Would you discovered he also can moreover have a mind harm that triggers all his troubles?"

This became what a BPD 17-yr-vintage boy's parents favored to understand. If the toddler does not increase and then modifications within the actions after a head trauma, no easy answer as to whether or not or now not or now not the conduct adjustments due to a head harm in infancy, including James. Nevertheless, because the mind right away regulates the movements and outcomes of BPD, it's miles useful to apprehend mind anatomy.

Some researchers don't forget the behavioral issues of BPD are within the ordinary operation of the two essential thoughts areas, frontal lobes and the limbic machine, and the hypothalamic-hypo bodily adrenal axis in a single community. We're going to talk approximately every body in flip.

Quick Anatomy Lesson

Approximately 3 pounds of mind weight. The mind stem, which contains bundles of nerve cells or neurons, connects to the spinal cord. Most of the cortex is called the mind. The outer layer of the mind is referred to as the cerebral cortex, that is only a few millimeters thick (along with the pores and skin of an apple), which includes as lots as one hundred thousand billion involved cells. The brain is cut up into 4 lobes, referred to as the frontal, parietal, temporal, and occipital lobes. Each lobe manages the ones behaviours.

The hippocampus and the amygdala are deep in the brain, beneath the temporal lobe. The vital obligation of the hippocampus is studying, and complicated varieties of memory and we're in a position to speak about the amygdala's characteristic later. The time lobe itself includes the a part of the thoughts that offers with listening to and sound and speech processing.

The occipital-lobe in the again of the mind includes the seen cortex, which recognizes and translates signs from the eyes. Our emphasis can be on brain regions which accumulate the finest hobby in BPD: the amygdala and the prefrontal cortex (PFC).

The Frontal Lobes and Trauma

Frontal lobes shape part of the government characteristic of the thoughts. It consists of the potential to do the following:

Recognize future results springing up from present moves

Choose amongst proper and horrific behavior

Conservation and weight of opposing viewpoints

Suppress and override undesirable social reactions

Determine similarities and discrepancies among occasions

People who suffered accidents or incidents that weakened their frontal lobes often display off irritability, impulsiveness and rage.

The limbic tool is part of the thoughts which often is called the "emotional mind" because it controls a number of our feelings and motivations, particularly the ones related to survival.

THE LIMBIC SYSTEM: MEMORY AND EMOTIONS

It is likewise the part of the mind that video display gadgets the reaction to combat or flight. The hippocampus and the amygdala are the two important factors of the limbic device. Amygdala plays an important feature in emotions like anxiety, rage and sexual behaviour. The amygdala additionally allows to create memories, in particular memories related to sturdy emotions. As Kathleen, a fairly touchy 17-twelve months-antique with BPD, began out to get maintain of counseling she regarded committed and seduced, however Kathleen refused to talk even as her mother attended the remedy. She expressed deep affection for her mother in man or woman periods, and her behavior have end up complex at the same time as her mom changed into in the house. Her mom stated she and Kathleen were extremely close to till Kathleen become 14. That emerge as on the identical time as the mom of Kathleen lost her very very very own mom to maximum cancers. She stated that Kathleen became associated with her own family, however she seemed to have dealt with the shortage of her grandmother as masses as possible. Kathleen labored in treatment to experience and tolerate her emotions without turning into self-adverse.

One day in counseling, we pointed out Kathleen's principle that the troubles had commenced throughout the time of the loss of life of her grandma, and the way Kathleen and her mom were very close before. He determined he changed into near together together with her parents. "What befell then?"I went to my mother and gave her a hug whilst my grandmother died. My mother wept and modified into so indignant. As she cried, she mentioned her mother, how empty she felt, she misplaced everything, and now she did not have really anybody. Kathleen said, at the same time as she heard her mom say she did not have all and sundry, she felt that she come to be harm extra than ever before. How may additionally additionally want to her mom don't forget she did now not have all of us? Kathleen, she had her. She had her. How can she say something like that? Whenever Kathleen saw her mother cry, her mom's memory may want to cause that she had no individual. This recollection changed into tied to effective and insupportable emotions of loneliness and sadness that led Kathleen to engage in self-damaging behavior as a way to deal with her sorrow. She had in no way cautioned her mother and had extra than three years of suffering with the memory and related emotions. When she emerge as prepared to tell her mom at remaining, her mom shattered and shouted, "You have been suffering good-bye! Why have not you ever suggested me that? Obviously, I did not imply I have become from you on my own. When 14, the amygdala and the hippocampus of Kathleen held her recollections of her mother's words and the autobiography was related to the sensation of ache, sorrow and distress. In evaluation with those with out BPD, the most constant locating in imagery research are improved hobby in amygdala, specifically when suicidal questioning is also professional. It is there critical to find out a way to lessen this behaviour to lower the waft of consistent emotions in BPD.

THE INTERPLAY

The the the the front lobes and the limbic gadget normally have interaction constantly. The hassle is that the the the front lobes, which manage preference-making, are near down in a notably emotional state of affairs and the limbic device this is concerned in feelings takes over. This response works in competition to human beings with BPD — or all of us. In BPD, as an example, it's miles almost not possible to suppose what the potential result of repetitive self-damage actions, which encompass cuts, finally of an episode of feeling crushed and self-injured. In BPD treatment, techniques aimed each at spotting and reducing excessive emotional conditions are essential. For them, BPD more youthful humans can spend more time of their frontal (rational) brains and train them to manipulate disputes higher.

THE PITUITARY-HYPOTHALAMIC–ADRENAL AXIS

A complicated institution of nerves that function in the rhythm of hypothalamus (which regulates the temperature, urge for food, thirst, and body rhythms), the hypophysical gland (which secretes hormones and oxytocin — that is vital within the dating among mom and infant), and the adrenal glands (this is chargeable for strain) The interplay a few of the ones 3 bodies, through neurotransmitter and hormones, regulates strain responses, governs early mother-infant attachment and regulates temper and sexuality.

Several research have tested that this nerve network in people with BPD does no longer art work properly, and treatments for those problems are focused. Some individuals who be by way of BPD, for instance, can take drug treatments that partly save you the effects of adrenaline which can reduce strain.

WHAT THE BRAIN REVEALS ABOUT BPD

Researchers of the University of Freiburg in Germany reviewed the posted neuroimaging and BPD findings in 2006. They stated that neuroimaging has grow to be one of the most essential contraptions for studies into the natural motives of BPD. Both imagery and BPD assessments confirmed adjustments in limbial device and frontal lobes, which the researchers felt have been everyday with the concept that mind problems make contributions to BPD signs and symptoms and symptoms.

Some human beings frequently request from me if this form of thoughts experiment or blood take a look at could in all likelihood "display" that someone has BPD or at the least "mistake his thoughts," as one determine placed it. The brief answer is that there aren't any current BPD checks. The longer solution, researchers have a look at data from extremely good varieties of scans to appearance if variations between the brains of BPD and BPD-loose ladies and men may be detected. Such scans have proven to this point what researchers expect — that the the the the front lobes and limblc tool play a high position in BPD.

WHY BPD BRAINS ARE DIFFERENT

The sixteen-year-antique Charles, a excessive faculty trainer, came into therapy due to the fact he had problem controlling his anger. He did nicely within the lecture room, but he exploded with close to friends and dates while he felt that matters had been no longer going his manner or that humans have been no longer trustworthy. He admitted that he had screamed at friends a few instances and physical attacked his woman friend in desperate moments. She isn't any precise from many teenagers who come to peer us due to the impulsive or aggressive method to others or themselves. Behaviours which encompass self-mutilation, bodily violence, attack, belongings destruction and drug use are the simplest subject of BPD that is well explored in era. In a 1996 have a have a examine of violent and impulsive firing sellers, forty seven% were determined to be recognized with a individual infection— specially borderline and anti-social individual issues. In a few other have a have a study, male home violence perpetrators had been much more likely than men who did not have interaction in domestic violence to have identified BPD. Brain scans display lower degrees of interest within the prefrontal cortex (PFC) in humans with impulsive aggression. This manner that the PFC is not so active in humans with impulsive aggression. Many thoughts scanning research show that people with BPD are disordered inside the PFC in assessment to the ones with out BPD, specially even as additionally they be via submit-demanding stress illness (PTSD). Like I said previously, having a far a good deal much less active PFC approach being capable of manage emotions (which incorporates anger) extra difficultly in the amygdala. Ultimately, all neuroimaging studies factors to amygdala and the prefrontal cortex troubles in human beings with BPD. This is however to be seen whether or now not these anomalies cause BPD or if BPD contributes to those abnormalities.

ENVIRONMENTAL AND BIOLOGICAL FACTOR

Dialectic conduct remedy (DBT) principle is that the reason and endurance of BPD are embedded in a hyper-sensitive neurobiological mechanism that interacts with environmental elements. In BPD, hypersensitive reaction will become complex if the person can't manipulate his or her feelings. The natural motives of hypersensitivity can be because of genetics, pre-born intrauterine and/or early developmental trauma, together with all kinds of abuse.

Environmental factors embody all conditions that penalize, traumatize or overpower this emotional vulnerability and are taken into consideration a crippling surroundings. The DBT model hypothesizes that BPD is due to a biological-environmental interaction over time which may additionally have a look at multiple tips. In some times, environmental have an effect on is extra; in others, natural have an effect on is greater crucial. The prevent cease end result, BPD is caused by the interplay of these elements in order that the character in no way learns to manipulate his or her emotions on the equal time as the surroundings turns into extra disruptive.

ROLE OF PARENTING

The seventeen-12 months-antique mom with BPD who had moved out of her mother and father ' homes once you have got abortion as quickly as said to me, "I am so sorry my circle of relatives is shattered. In months, my daughter hasn't been speakme to her father or me. He's furious about how she treats me. I'm however dissatisfied with my two more younger children. I'm tired and depressed, no longer thinking that I even have lots fight left in me. I need to be thrilled with my daughter. I'd want to attain her out and help her in conjunction with her ache. I failed her as a little one, and now, as an person, I fail her. I'm moreover concerned approximately what will take place to different kids. "Getting proper right into a" blame activity "isn't useful for the treatment of BPD teenagers or their families. There is usually a lot of blame on one in every of a kind humans as regards to BPD and it's miles clean to get stuck within the debate of "horrific parenting." In nearly each case, parents did their great. It ought to now be clear that BPD has many hazard elements and reasons. That said, parenting will play a element inside the development of BPD — on occasion a huge position. Understanding the characteristic of parental schooling allows us to pick out the threat factors and encourages the family to adjust anything fashion of parental care contributes.

A cutting-edge-day study located that insufficient parental and stressful reports need to adversely have an effect on the law of mood. The researchers positioned that individuals who perceived their mother and father as horrific mother and father had trouble describing their feelings and prolonged depression. However, even though there has been additionally sexual abuse, a actually perceived motherly parenting fashion changed into determined to help teens explicit emotion.

The researchers concluded that the know-how of parenting abilties changed into vital in the improvement of unable to precise feelings. It was additionally determined that one decide's first-class parenthood have to save you the development of alexithymia (disability to define feelings, in special terms, someone feels) if the parentage of the opportunity decide have grow to be appeared as non-maximum beneficial.

TEMPERAMENT AND ATTACHMENT

The term of temperament psychology is usually considered to be the hereditary basis of the person, the herbal, inborn trouble of a person's man or woman. Of instance, parents can also offer an cause of how their kids variety and apprehend these differences in the first 12 months. Besides temperament, a amazing deal of research and reflected picture now takes area on attachment deficits in the youth of adults with BPD. Attachment is virtually a choice to are searching out closeness and sense stable at the same time as the man or woman is gift. It is the emotional bond that persists over the years and on this precise context connects a infant alongside together with his mother, dad or awesome caregivers. A primary concept of attachment is that responsive and customized responses of a decide to a little one's needs bring about a normal attachment and an risky attachment because of a lack of such appropriate response. It stays to be visible whether or not or now not poor attachment of the decide to the infant is a reason of BPD or whether or not damaged thoughts wiring consequences in terrible attachment. Nevertheless, horrific attachment is an nearly trendy finding in BPD studies.

PARENT-CHILD BOND

The outstanding of maternal care has been tested again and again to are watching for the safety of infants. The touchy responsiveness of the discern is appeared because the number one determinant of whether or now not or not a toddler is stable. Studies have validated that horrible parental persona characteristics are related to infant loss of self warranty. Negative parenting traits encompass, as an instance, tension, black-and-white thinking, loss of empathy, outsourcing blame to others, especially to the kid, and the perception that every one of their movements are within the pleasant interests of a little one. Research indicates that the empathy and openness of dad and mom to their children makes conversation with others less complex and that strong connection makes this all less difficult. Disturbed attachment may additionally want to have a prime function in the improvement of BPD, but research have validated, collectively with all genetic and neurological consequences, that as a exceptional deal as 87% of patients with BPD who required hospitalization for their symptoms had a data of sizeable violence and/or forget about and the 80 one% were unnoticed thru their mother and father. The hassle of trauma is essential due to the reality research have proven that youth trauma impacts the functioning of the frontal lobe this is involved in BPD pathology. Nonetheless, it's far crucial to test the location of parenting.

WHY EARLY ATTACHMENT IS VERY IMPORTANT

Karlen Lyons-Ruth of Harvard Medical School of Cambridge Hospital has labored on the early attachment between toddler and caregiver to the later improvement of persona. She has researched the relationship amongst early attachment and care extraordinary and character borderline symptomatology. Lyons-Ruth emphasized the significance of mom-child critiques, which contribute to a little one's capability to manipulate emotions. He theorizes that "bonding-exploration equilibrium" disturbance interferes with a little one's cognitive and social capability growth. The connection-exploration balance is the idea that if a little one is to find out their surroundings very well, they need to be rest assured that their mother might be there if there is a risk. A little one who isn't always confident that this can take region makes a speciality of her mother's attachment in location of on her environment. The worry that your mom could not be present if a danger arises corresponds to the fears of later abandonment in BPD sufferers.

In 1991, Lyons-Ruth and her colleagues endorsed numerous research displaying that maternal, family danger factors together with infant abuse, parental strain and the depressing symptoms of mothers continually produced youngsters who observed it tough to form a secure attachment to their caregivers.

A 2004 assessment of thirteen BPD attachment research decided that each have a take a look at concluded that there is a sturdy hyperlink amongst BPD and prone attachment. The most common kinds of attachment for BPD subjects are unresolved, demanding and concerned attachments. The analysis decided that sufferers displayed a choice for affection and challenge for vulnerability and rejection in every of these kinds of attachments. The authors concluded that the identification of volatile relationships in adults with BPD is consistent with the locating of dysfunctional interpersonal relationship with BPD. They furthermore concluded that people with volatile attachments are susceptible to BPD boom.

ON GENES AND INHERITANCE

Most dad and mom anticipate their little one's BPD must be associated with their genes, either doing a little factor wrong or passing a awful gene. In addition, few adoptive dad and mom apprehend that during accompanied youngsters, critical behavioral and character issues may additionally moreover occur. When such problems stand up, dad and mom are often accountable and be given as real with that they may be responsible. BPD signs and signs and symptoms and symptoms–specially inadequate frustration, mood swings, paranoia/dissociation, impulsiveness, and extreme, volatile relationships–are extra commonplace among partner and children of borderline patients than those of various persona sicknesses. It additionally seems that during first-degree relations (i.E. Dad and mom, circle of relatives, and descendants) of BPD patients, BPD signs and signs— in vicinity of BPD itself — are greater well-known. Family and dual studies of BPD mean that whilst some behaviors which consist of impulsivity, suicide, temper instability and aggressiveness do seem to be inherited at the same time as BPD itself can not be inherited. Most mother and father apprehend, for example, that they may be moody as kids, but now not so moody as their infant. Some dad and mom admit that they had suicidal mind, however they in no way did. In view of the remarkable variability in BPD behaviour, it's miles possible that many genes will form a part of the complex puzzle. However, there has no longer been a research that decided a gene causing BPD; however, studies show that gene variations can be strongly associated with advantageous behaviors. When blended with mind anatomy and the effects of the surroundings on someone, those gene variations will provide a extra entire answer.

BEHAVIORAL SYMPTOMS AND GENES

The crucial BPD and genetic research investigated ninety two same and 129 non-identical Norwegian dual pairs. The equal genes and the same putting are common to identical twins. Twins that aren't equal proportion the identical surroundings, but do now not have the equal genes. Researchers discovered that 69 percent of the signs and symptoms of BPD had been genes and the very last 31 percentage had been environmental elements. Most researchers take delivery of as proper with that BPD is approximately 60% genetic and 40% environmental.

John Gunderson, MD, and his fellow researchers at McLean Hospital in Belmont, Massachusetts, have completed a big take a look at into BPD genetics. His institution divided BPD sufferers into three subtypes based totally on the number one problems displayed through manner of the use of each organization. There are temper swings within the first group, behavioral issues inside the second one like self-harm, and interpersonal issues like hard relationships in the 1/3 one. The investigators study whether or not or not this sort of subtypes has a stronger genetic issue than the opposite. The look at hopes to provide consequences so as to assist us further classify BPD and increase a gene financial group for destiny BPD studies (in which DNA is accrued and stored). A have a observe of BPD determined out model in a dopamine gene, the brain chemistry that regulates movement, emotion, motivation, and pride sensations. Patients with BPD appear like more traumatic than sufferers without this genetic abnormality.

OTHER FACTORS IN THE DEVELOPMENT OF BPD

While attachment troubles are just a few or low serotonin degrees which have had an impact at the improvement of BPD, there are numerous parent commands and serotonin booster remedy which is probably all required.

Substance Abuse

Dawn Thatcher, Ph.D, and buddies investigated adolescent alcohol and distinctive adolescent inclinations as predictors of character BPD symptoms in 2005. Substance abuse Researchers recruited in their research 355 young adults with a statistics of alcohol abuse and 169 young adults with out a information of alcohol abuse. Six years later, BPD signs and signs and symptoms and signs have been assessed in young adults. Researchers determined that young adults with drug dependancy and one of a kind psychiatric problems are much more likely to growth person BPD than teenagers with alcohol-free psychiatric issues.

Sexual Abuse, Maltreatment, and Trauma

Lots of research have demonstrated that the majority of people coping with individual troubles have a history of trauma, neglect and violence. This is in particular proper of humans with BPD diagnoses. Adults with BPD and a information of children's and adolescent bodily abuse are twice as possibly as people with out BPD or an abusive records to revel in submit-annoying strain ailment (PTSD). Clinicians who address BPD often looking for early life abuse, and once they find it, they tie it proper right into a affected man or woman's reason of BPD. The BPD literature strongly endorses this perception, which suggests that maximum people with BPD have suffered highbrow, bodily and sexual violence. Research suggests that as much as seventy five% of BPD patients had been sexually abused, and it's far important that many are abused. Nevertheless, a huge minority has no longer suffered sexual abuse in childhood. Gunderson located out that sexual abuse isn't always suitable or essential to set off BPD. Evidence has moreover established that sexual abuse of a determine is substantially linked to little one suicide and is notably related to self-mutilation, each parental sexual violence and emotional overlook about.

The following listed 4 factors regarding abuse have been located to be essential predictors of BPS analysis:

Emotional denial via a male caregiver

Inconsistency in treatment with the aid of the usage of a woman caregiver

Female gender

Sexual abuse with the useful resource of using a male non-caregiver

Of sufferers with BPD who have been sexually abused, extra than 50 percentage disclose violence each in youngsters and youngsters, on at least one danger factors had been counseled as essential predictors for BPD diagnostics. More than 50% additionally declare that their harassment includes the use of force or violence in as a minimum one form of penetration. It is cheap that the severity of the sexual abuse suggested in kids is extensively associated with the general severity of BPD and its desired functioning.

Childhood Mental Disorders

Nearly all teenagers referred to in our McLean Hospital unit were identified with distinct intellectual situations, which includes tension, melancholy, bipolar illness, PTSD, ADD and lots of others. Childhood intellectual issues, which embody ADD, ADHD, or bipolar disease will boom the danger that the affected baby can also expand a individual illness even as he or she grows up. This may be executed in unique ways.

First, the circumstance itself ought to at once affect the improvement of character. For example, a infant who's depressed can experience worthless, and that feeling can grow to be a middle belief over time that they've about themselves. Second, the symptoms and moves of a sickness can bring about a reaction by means of the use of others that could effect the improvement of the persona. For example, a hyperactive infant can be physical punished or abused in young adults thru a teen figure's ninety six Borderline character illness or get preserve of extraordinary responses, on occasion being punished, occasionally overlooked. Thirdly, it is possible that youngsters mental disorder is inside the first location surely a manifestation of person problems. Australia psychiatrist Joseph Rey, MD, has performed various studies over time and is one of the most important researchers in person development in adolescence. His business organization discovered that forty percentage of sufferers recognized in puberty were later diagnosed with a individual sickness with a "disruptive disorder" (along side ADHM). Just 12 percent of sufferers with intellectual (or temper) problems, which consist of melancholy, have a contamination in their character. When he continued to comply with this institution of youngsters into adulthood, the dearth of functioning became related to a persona ailment. Issues blanketed criminal troubles, negative paintings statistics, early coexistence, social isolation and interpersonal courting issues.

Other research has discovered that persona troubles are greater than double the everyday in people who have adolescent temper, tension and drug abuse troubles; and the greater axis I cope with someone, the more likely it will become to boom a ailment of personality.

Online Danger

The Internet offers a sturdy advantage to society, but there are many threats there and teenagers with BPD are specially inclined. Online sexual predators, drug and suicide records, unrelated friendships, the advent of immediate pals and hastily disseminate nameless bullying are just some of the risks.

For instance, research in 2014 suggests that cyberbullying is toward children and youth' suicidal wondering than conventional bullying. Cyberbullying these days is feasible on some of systems, like boards, webpages of social networking (e.G., Facebook, Instagram, Twitter), on-line video games, and textual content messages. The extensive style of cyberbullying youngsters and kids stages among 10 and 40 percentage depending on the age corporation. A collection of articles titled Children, Adolescents and the Internet were published with the resource of the American Psychological Association (APA) in April 2006. The APA cited that "seventy five-90% of children inside the USA use the Internet for e-mail, instantaneous conversation (IM), visit chat rooms and discover different net web sites at the World Wide Web," and that "plenty time on the Web will have every awful and excessive best effects on younger human beings, for example sharing self-injurious enjoy with some humans, and the educational and health consequences. The have a have a study additionally determined that the frequency and tone of feedback on their profiles affects their self-esteem. Positive comments boosted the vanity and well-being of younger human beings, even as bad comments did the opportunity.

The Internet can be specifically crucial for marginalized teens. It gives an area in which they feel that they will be at low threat to satisfy others who percentage their versions (perceived and actual) and to change records which may be difficult to percent in character. The net moreover offers anonymity; teenagers can disguise inside the lower back of intended identities. Studies show that social help and alienation are the crucial element purpose for becoming a member of an internet discussion board. Unfortunately, younger people with psychological problems are more likely than without this shape of problems to percentage private information on the Internet with absolute aliens. For instance, research have verified that almost all of self-damage boards and boards are ruled via way of women most of the some time of 12 - 20. You check in to request and percent information on cutting and special self-injurious behavior. True, the ones channels assist marginalized more youthful human beings socially and emotionally, however they normalize reducing, remarkable self-injurious movements and doubtlessly lethal "problem solving" solutions. Anonymously on an Internet talk board, the subsequent message have become posted: "Thank you men. Whenever I bypass nuts, I join up. It does not even get my buddies. Chatting with a number of you is exquisite. This lets in me to apprehend and I am regarding what some of you've got had been given completed. Having BPD is an lousy detail to be dealt with and maximum of the time I revel in isolated. Someone said cutting, but I do not cut. Someone said slicing. Alternatively, I burn and frequently experience empty, but burning additionally lets in. I definitely have spent all my existence in the health facility and in emergency rooms, putting aside maximum of my circle of relatives and pals. I need to discover those who percent my state of affairs". In a piece of writing entitled The Digital Cutting Edge: The Internet and Adolescent Self-Injury, researchers looked at the feature of the Internet message boards in the development of self-injurious agencies. In 1998, they determined that a message board with almost 100 customers modified into set up to cope with self-damage. In 2005, 168 boards had almost 10,000 human beings. The boards provided open forums wherein human beings felt they have been heard. One crucial query is: What happens to emotionally insecure, Internet-primarily based youngsters, or to on line existence that provide little continuity or structure?

Who does ask for help once they have problem?

Online forums are an impersonal alternative for circle of relatives and pals. The Internet is not whole of those who recognize the state of affairs or the whole suffering of a person who asks for help. One of the most important fears of BPD sufferers is loss. For example, if you're on line, it's miles easy to log off at the same time as the communication is just too severe.

This can motive feelings of separation if a person with BPD seeks help and the pair logs off online. One 16-year-vintage woman advocated me if she advised a supportive peer on an internet speak board that she concept of suicide, the character would virtually not solution or disconnect. She felt deserted via manner of someone she just did not understand. "I've been cyber-dumped," she stated. Nevertheless, the Internet offers advantages. Since on-line boards and blogs can, in principle, be an area in which less socially professional younger humans percentage anonymously opinions, they can also be an area for teens to attach. Researchers have positioned that such on line exchanges lessen social isolation among children and permit them to talk and discover their identity. This will make clean how the Internet can end up a digital peer help community for depressed young adults, a place to precise their emotions and to exchange records approximately coping strategies. In addition to normalizing online businesses, self-injurious and lifestyles-threatening behaviour. We offer a effective vehicle to carry self-injurious young adults collectively. In the 1980s anorexia nervosa modified into commonplace rapid after it grow to be found as an trouble to the mass media. For example, in a 2002 look at via using Fijian youngsters, disorderly consuming became extensively extra commonplace after exposure to mass media. It changed into exacerbated by using manner of the usage of representations of feminine splendor with the useful resource of that e-mail. Another knowledgeable me that when a couple poster, "a mentor," as it come to be described, told the lady to inform the mom that she had taken an overdose of the drugs, it had stored her from the overdose. Nonetheless, some teens say they might in no way have had the idea of harming themselves had they not heard approximately it on line. In addition to using self-damage as a coping talent, many different online discussions are troubling, which includes approximately alcohol utilization, sexual behavior, food loss and suicide normalization. Another famous situation count number of teenagers communique is unhappiness with parents who, they are saying, do not understand.

Although controlling and regulating Internet and social media content material material and get right of entry to are increasingly difficult, dad and mom and caregivers want to undergo in thoughts that those are crucial statistics property for more younger humans. Some on-line property are valuable, however others are incomplete, misinformed and probably deadly. A extra youthful person desires an area, whether or not or not or no longer in counseling or with a decide, in which she or he will be capable of inquire what they have got a look at or pay interest. To dad and mom, interest without judgment is the maximum critical ability to learn. It's an functionality that requires extraordinary practice.

Cultural and Societal Concerns and BPD

You simply want to check any grocery keep's test-out alley to appearance that what you promote is a way of life that encourages a' fake self' with tooth snap shots, splendor over your brains, and intercourse with out engagement. (The faux self happens at the identical time as human beings are compelled to meet external necessities, together with to be terrible or adorable, whilst such expectations may be incompatible with who they sincerely are and the manner they could generally behave or enjoy. Otherwise, dwelling in a everlasting faux self-popularity can turn out to be relatively risky because of the truth human beings lose their experience in their actual self.) One expression is "better chemistry," or the belief that a pill will enhance things. While this is in particular true in many cases, it does not paintings for masses others. Saying to humans with the BPD that there can be a smooth answer or "snapping it out" invalidates their know-how. The stress and strain on college students (in themselves, mother and father, and institutions of higher education) to carry out and succeed is some other component in cutting-edge life that contributes to growing

BPD. Most clinics say that self-harm in reaction to stress is growing appreciably.

A vital take a look at in 2011 placed that of the 11,529 responding college college students, 15.Three percent registered self-injury and 6.Eight percentage had self-injured sooner or later of the preceding 12 months. Most college students who had self-injured said self-injuries greater than as soon as and nearly half of of greater than six instances. The common age of self-damage initiation have turn out to be 15.2 years. Numerous of these cultural factors integrate to create the situations for BPD's boom with the family environment and human biology.

The Bottom Line

BPD is a multifaceted contamination with many components that help to shape it. Research has severa hyperlinks and alternatives. These encompass genes in impulsive conduct and mood disturbance, have extended neurotransmitter stages inside the BPD brains and abuse victims, and display compromised or underdeveloped regions of BPD in advantageous thoughts areas. Instead, the affect of horrible parenthood, damaged determination, sexual abuse, invalidation, drug abuse influences and, ultimately, the stresses of current way of life. BPD is consequently not added on with the beneficial useful resource of 1 factor. Alternatively, the cumulative outcomes on the developing thoughts, its structures and chemistry of the surroundings and the genes draw collectively the scientific photograph.

The downside is that BPD develops over time and regularly needs years of recovery treatment. Nonetheless, it is promising that there are various strategies, and these interventions will hold to decorate through the years.

Chapter 6: Treatment Of Borderline Personality Disorder

A evaluation may be lovable, disappointing or annoying for borderline person sickness. But BPD reacts without a doubt to treatment, however the effect it is able to have on a person's life. Those who are suffering need to expect permanent comfort if they come out of the shadows to are searching out help. Psychotherapy, it's normally complemented by a combination of medicine, talents education, and holistic healing strategies, restores health and energy, is the cornerstone of BPD remedy plans.

Getting a Diagnosis

A borderline character ailment (BPD) analysis can be a hard proposition for specialists of intellectual health. Its signs and symptoms and symptoms in part overlap with wonderful intellectual contamination, its prevalence has prolonged for the purpose that been underestimated and frequently develops inside the presence of similar or conflicting signs and symptoms and signs that can complicate assessment.

However, as soon as an accurate diagnosis for BPD has been made, there are fantastic opportunities for recuperation. BPD patients seeking out professional assist might also additionally have get proper of get right of entry to to with a showed record of fulfillment to expert remedy options and top notch treatment strategies.

BPD Treatment Program

Until care starts offevolved for borderline persona illness, a scientific expert is probably appointed to supervise and co-ordinate the overall affected individual rehabilitation software program. Objectives or goals are generated to encourage the affected man or woman to make certain a regular restoration price. Healing programs are tailored to contain new processes or techniques at the same time as there may be development or no longer.

Although individuals are precise, the overall shape of a BPD restoration plan normally consists of the following crucial tendencies:

Individual, organization and family psychotherapy. Drug-focused care has become the norm for plenty styles of intellectual contamination, with the assist of therapy. But the equation is reversed with BPD. Therapy stays the center of all BPD remedy plans and particular healing techniques to deal with the singular signs and symptoms of this distinctly not unusual circumstance had been superior.

Medication. There are not any tablets mainly designed for borderline person troubles. Nevertheless, prescribed drugs continue to be available to assist improve the consequences or underlying conditions of BPD.

Life talents training and education. Classroom training which give patients with statistics at the specifics in their highbrow health problems and/or teaching them a manner to cope with signs and associated lifestyles complications have now end up famous within the remedy of highbrow fitness regimes.

Holistic techniques of healing. Included further to extra traditional remedy patterns, holistic mind-body techniques are useful to patients with BPD for 2 motives— to start with because of the fact they help lessen pressure; and secondly, because of the reality they can assist people to extend greater willpower.

Additional remedy services for health issues co-happening. If exceptional highbrow fitness issues or drug use troubles are recognized, remedy programs have to deal with those issues concurrently with their hobby to BPD signs and symptoms.

Persons with borderline suicidal character disorder may be forced to be hospitalized in psychiatric care till the crisis passes, or be troubled via immoderate episodes of dissociative symptoms and signs.

Different Types of Therapy for Borderline Personality Disorder (BPD)

Psychotherapy is a core of a borderline persona contamination healthcare software program in each outpatients and inpatients. The majority of men and women on the lookout for BPD care will acquire affected individual, network and family counseling, with everyday periods in which required.

While each considered one in every of them has numerous first rate variations, as a minimum one or types of psychotherapy are part of the maximum famous remedy plans:

Dialectic Behavioural Therapy (DBT)

 Considering the gold desired in BPD treatment, DBT turn out to be specially designed to cope with this situation. This remedy teaches capabilities in emotional law, stress manage, interest and self-self belief and interpersonal communique with a realistic guidance that specialize in commonplace fitness and great of life.

Mentalization-Based Therapy (MBT)

The mentalization-primarily based treatment is designed to enhance the potential of BPD sufferers to hyperlink their emotions and behavior with particular highbrow states not only in themselves, but in others. Another remedy that is designed for BPD sufferers. With this understanding in hand, patients can begin to recognize their scenario as a prelude to their eventual restoration.

Cognitive Behavioral Therapy (CBT)

Cognitive behavioral treatment is a key problem of most treatment strategies for mental health, collectively with the ones which give help to people with borderline personality disorder. During those remedy sessions, patients are taught to transform negative kinds of thinking into extra great and fantastic states of mind until the ones conduct are installed.

Eye-Movement Desensitization and Reprocessing (EMDR)

Through physical movement and intellectual hobby, EMDR remedy permits patients with intellectual health problems to address previous traumas appropriately and in an surroundings that focuses completely on fitness and healing.

Transference-Focused-Psychotherapy (TFP)

In this remedy, the point of interest is on building a powerful, sympathetic courting among the affected character and the therapist, then serving as a version for the affected individual's behavioral and intellectual reconstruction.

Schema-Focused-Psychotherapy (SFT)

The creative form of psychotherapy helps patients deal with their troubles through alternating among 5 modes or regimes that define the BPD affected person's underlying character (steady with SFT precept): deserted and compelled babies, aggrieved and impulsive youngsters, the unconditional protector, punitive dad and mom and healthy adults.

Systems-Training-For-Emotional-Predictability and Problem-Solving (STEPPS)

This is a 20-week outpatient company remedy initiative that mixes cognitive-behavioural restructuring and training in workout-orientated talents. The training commands include circle of relatives participants and buddies to help BPD patients extend a sturdy network of helpers and caregivers.

Family Psycho-schooling

This treatment gives the cherished ones of BPD sufferers with steerage, information and emotional aid to their gain and to make sure their entire co-operation inside the illness recuperation application.

Additional Therapies For Co-Occurring Disorders

If co-happening troubles are diagnosed, remedy is also vital. Integrated intellectual or behavioral fitness remedy applications are designed especially for managing more than one troubles simultaneously, and the bulk of remedies inside a massive BPD treatment programme may be correctly tailor-made to address distinct highbrow fitness troubles.

BPD MEDICATIONS

No mainly advanced capsules for the remedy of borderline persona disorder. Two pharmaceutical commands are but capable of combating the most disabling BPD signs: mood stabilizers and antipsychotics.

Antipsychotics-are normally prescribed for schizophrenia, however on the same time as administered in lower doses, the intensity of the cognitive and perceptual distortions which BPD patients frequently enjoy can be reduced. Extreme thoughts, paranoia and dissociative episodes can drastically disrupt guys's and ladies's lives, however antipsychotics can help them in dealing with those symptoms and reconnecting with realities.

Mood stabilizers are the drugs of choice for BPD folks who combat impulsivity and are emotionally uncovered. They can make a contribution to reducing the depth of BPD explosive anger humans and can counter the disabled tension, it's so frequently a companion of this all-encompassing intellectual fitness ailment.

Skills Training, Holistic Healing Process, and Education

Most BPD sufferers take benefit of advanced skills schooling packages that educate them the strategies to address the symptom of BPD. Having strength of mind skills are essential for the protection and well-being of humans with highbrow fitness problems because of the fact the medication do not constantly feature and therapists are not available 24 hours a day outside of the residential treatment facility.

In the intervening time, information instructions can assist human beings with limited person problems advantage an know-how in their conditions, clarifying misconceptions that can save you them from committing themselves to recuperation. However, the knowledge they advantage approximately BPD can help them in early-degree to apprehend signs and provide them with a miles higher idea of wherein they stand on the continuum of borderline person disorders.

In residential mental fitness facilities, holistic intellectual-frame restoration techniques are routinely available in recent times and may in truth be of benefit to human beings with BPD throughout ambulatory packages. People with this illness have hassle dealing with their emotions and holistic practices are designed to cope with this particular trouble.